Whittle Your Ears

WHITTLE YOUR EARS

POEMS, SONGS AND PLAYS FOR CHILDREN

by

Barbara Dawson Betteridge

Printed through support from the Betteridge Family

Title: *Whittle Your Ears*
Author: Barbara Dawson Betteridge
Advisors: Jonitha Hasse, Helen Lubin, Samuel Glaze
Editor: David Mitchell
Cover Layout: Hallie Wootan
Cover Artist: Jason Healy
Proofreader: Ann Erwin
ISBN # 1-888365-68-4
© 2005 by: AWSNA Publications
        3911 Bannister Road
        Fair Oaks, CA 95628

        916-961-0927
        www.awsna.org/publications
        publications@awsna.org

A PROMISE

Whittle your ears
if you would hear
whir of a beetle,
whuff of a deer,
butterfly ripping
a spider's web,
or bubble of crab
at tide's low ebb.

Whittle your ears
and sharpen your eyes
if you would find
where the falcon flies –
where under the ocean
the limpet lies –
And you'll never grow old;
You will only grow wise.

TABLE OF CONTENTS

PREFACE

Barbara Betteridge found her childhood friends mostly in nature and in books. Small wonder then that she achieved such a gift of writing of nature and heroes in poems and in plays for children.

Barbara never taught in a Waldorf school, but she watched Highland Hall grow from its infancy in 1953, watched the children grow, and supported the teachers with ideas, research, poems and verses, translations and class plays. The plays included in this book grew out of close collaboration with class teachers at Highland Hall. The closest working together was with Bertha Sharpe, who became a class teacher in 1959. From then until Bertha's death in 1978, these two women spoke together on the telephone nearly every day. Bertha was for Barbara eyes into the world of the school, the children, the challenges. Barbara was for Bertha the reflecting pool where Bertha could unload the day's burdens, reflect on them in the telling and receive inspiration and support, often in the form of poems and plays. Although other teachers also commissioned plays, the deep daily working was always with Bertha.

While Barbara's health kept her body homebound, her spirit would soar across the seas and into the hearts of human beings. She was well aware of her responsibility to produce plays of high literary quality to help "develop good taste and balance of soul." It was important to her that the language be beautiful, masterfully crafted, worthy to nourish as it is learned by heart. While writing some plays, she would get so engrossed in her work that she spoke of even the most mundane things in iambic pentameter. Barbara's plays have had a profound effect on the souls of children, those who lived into them through acting as well as those who watched them performed.

Mont Saint Michel and *Our Favorite Star* remind the young child that there are forces beyond the earthly who guide us and shape our world.

Grammar's Garden helps to lift into the realm of play the learning of grammar with its necessary form and rules.

The Magic Pitcher and *The Golden Fleece* reflect a stage of historical development when human beings took an active role in their own destinies, though still aware of divine interaction.

Meeting the world of science through clear observation, sixth graders still long for the imagery and hidden meaning of fairy tales. *The Castle of the Kingdom of the Stones*, bringing the study of mineralogy to life, meets these needs.

Boy-girl relationships, ideals of courtesy, constancy, courage and love are awakened and met in *The Sacred Flame*.

Long glorified as a hero, *Columbus* has come to be seen in a different, less favorable light. Should we abolish him from the curriculum or welcome the opportunity to discuss with more mature students of seventh or eighth grade the gifts and the shadow side of his role in history? As we face the doldrums or the stormy seas of life, can we remain true to our calling? Can we recognize the temptations, own the failures? When we travel to foreign lands or meet people of different cultures, do we open ourselves to the new or only transplant and impose the old views we bring with us? Greed, colonialism, exploitation, slavery, capitalism, lack of respect for other religions and peoples – perhaps looking at these forces in relation to Columbus can stimulate fruitful discussion of current events, foreign policy and relations with indigenous peoples of the world. May the *Columbus* play included here (written in 1950 and 1963) be seen not as a relic from the past, but as a contribution to a more balanced view of a man who struggled to follow his individual strivings within the social and economic circumstances of his time.

The Other Wise Man is a dramatic rendering of Henry van Dyke's timeless story, deeply moving, beautifully written, soul nourishing.

Thanks to Hiebel and the Starke family, for permission to publish Barbara's translations and dramatizations of their works, to John Brousseau for supplying *The Golden Fleece*, to Samual Glaze for help with selection, to Helen Lubin for selection and editing, to Channa Andriesse Seidenberg for her knowledgeable and inspiring exposition on pentatonic music, to Ute Brewer and Christine Hasse for typing, and especially to David Mitchell of AWSNA Publications for his patience and encouragement to bring about this volume.

As Barbara wrote most of these works as gifts to the children of Highland Hall School, we publish them now as a gift to children throughout and beyond the Waldorf School Movement. May they continue to inspire and enrich the lives of children.

– Jonitha Hasse
Hillsdale, NY
Spring 2005

Poems

The Children's Poems

One of the foremost signatures of a living education is the presence of the spoken word. The young, growing human being's experience of discovering and embracing but also being held by the world is supported and furthered by well-spoken language, both as it lives in the human environment and in the child's own activity. This engagement with the living word cultivates the ongoing conversation between the individual and the world.

It is fortunate that in Waldorf schools there is a time in the rhythmic part of the main lesson for daily speech practice. This may consist of exercises as well as poetry – a practice of hearing, speaking, listening, and, above all, of bringing one's attention and full inner activity into meaningful engagement with the spoken word. At every stage, this needs to be age-appropriate and purposeful, supporting and furthering our pedagogical intentions.

The choice of poetry needs to take both thematic as well as artistic considerations into account. While the theme may be related to the season, to the main lesson subject, or to another relevant situation, it is through the artistic elements that aspects of the pedagogical gesture become effective. These elements include, for example, rhythm, rhyme and other sound qualities, the movement of the thought thread or of the unfolding pictures, and the particular poetic style. In teacher education and professional development, learning how to work with these elements is a vital component of the overall task at hand.

The poems in this book are loosely arranged in age sequence. Choosing a poem will be done all the more wisely and sensitively if the teacher tries it out by alternately speaking it aloud and reading it silently several times, letting it interest the ear. We may begin to sense what is inwardly brought into movement and called upon in working with a particular piece.

This collection is a welcome addition to the fount of the daily water of life of which we partake in the spoken word. Be it the 'humble bumble bee a-humming,' the 'darn-darn-darning-needle,' 'an inch-worm stitch across a rose,' the 'artist Spring, errant thing,' or the 'fire-filled and fire-fed' hummingbird, all will whittle our ears for some of the more inaudible tidings that are the leaven for each growing life – each 'candle in the wind.'

– Helen Lubin
Sacramento, CA
Spring 2005

A PROMISE

Whittle your ears
if you would hear
whir of a beetle,
whuff of a deer,
butterfly ripping
a spider's web,
or bubble of crab
at tide's low ebb.

Whittle your ears
and sharpen your eyes
if you would find
where the falcon flies –
where under the ocean
the limpet lies –
And you'll never grow old,
You will only grow wise.

THE SNOWFLAKES

Waft we softly, lightly falling –
Leave the sky, for earth is calling!
Softly sift we o'er the mountains,
Fold the forest, fold the fountains.

Each of us a tiny star,
Sent to earth from heaven afar,
Weave a magic mantle even,
Soft and smooth as clouds in heaven.

STARS

Whenever we go to the desert,
I get to stay up late
And watch the sparkly stars come out
And hear them jubilate.

For if you're very quiet,
You can seem to hear them sing
Like angel voices far away,
Until the heavens ring.

GRACE

We thank the water, earth and air
And the helping powers they bear.
We thank the people, loving, good,
Who grow and cook our daily food.
And now at last we thank the Sun,
The Light and Life of every one.

GRACE

With every bite of bread
Think of the Sun's warm red
That on the budding grain has shone
And made it grow, from love.

With every bite of bread
Think of your brother's need
Who suffers hunger all alone.
Oh you who have God's blessing known,
Go, give him bread, and love.

Bei jedem Bissen Brot
Denk an der Sonne rot
Die Korn auf Körnlein hat erwärmt
Und wachsen liess aus Liebe.

Bei jedem Bissen Brot
Denk an des Bruders Not,
Der einsam sich am Hunger härmt.
O du den Gottes Segen wärmt,
Geh', gib ihm Brot und Liebe.

Martin Tittmann
Translated by BDB

A GRACE

For fruit and flower,
Leaf, stem and root
We thank thee, Father in heaven.

Grant us we pray
Strength for the day
And bring us home at even.

ADVENT GARDEN

Lo the angels through the windows
Of the crystals looking down,
See the fruits that have fallen,
See the apples on the ground.

They are seeking in the hearts
Of the people here on Earth –
They are looking for the Light,
For the Christ-Child come to birth.

CHRISTMAS

All the birds in Christendom
Were singing on this morn:
"Ti-rah-la-li! Ti-rah-la-la!
'Tis Christ our Lord is born!"

All the birds in Bethlehem
Were singing in their joy:
"Ti-rah-la-li! Ti-rah-la-la!
He's born, the wondrous Boy!"

All the birds around the world
Were singing with one voice:
"Ti-rah-la-li! Ti-rah-la-la!
The Babe is born!
            Rejoice!"

FUNNY BEE

A honey-bee, a funny bee,
in yellow velvet tights
visits all the garden flowers,
then on a ledge alights.

She looks at me inquiringly.
"Why do you think it odd
a bee should like to sit awhile
and just admire God?"

CRICKET IN A JAR

Was a cricket
in a thicket,
right outside my window-bar.

Pa and I went
out to find him,
popped him in a
pickle jar.

Now he sits
in satisfaction
snug upon
my window sill.

And when at night
I put the lights out,
brightly sings he,
loud and shrill.

DRAGONFLY

Darn – darn – darning-needle,
Zipping here and there,
What good is it to dart and weave?
You only mend thin air!

Darn – darn – darning-needle,
Perching on a rock –
Don't just sit there, darning-needle!
Come and mend my sock.

A MANTIS IS

A mantis is a twiggy beast
whose legs look much like litter.*
Though pill-bug stew's his favorite feast,
he'll snatch a lesser critter.

And when he has his dinner spread
(two bugs caught unawares),
he'll fold his feet and bow his head
and promptly say his prayers.

Litter: twigs and leaves on the forest floor

INCH-WORM

Did you ever watch an inch-worm
Stitch across a rose?
It's clear enough he's measuring
As loop-along he goes.
But what is so confusing
Is how the fellow knows
Which end's the one to follow –
Which is head and which is toes.

MR. ROBIN

"Doesn't it tickle your tongue,
Mr. Robin,
To carry a worm like that?
– I can see how he squiggles
And squirms and wiggles,
How squooshy he is and fat."
– Bird doesn't answer.
Bird doesn't stop.
Bird's in a hurry.
Worm's gonna drop.

ALARM CLOCK

"Chirp," says the robin,
"Cheep," says the wren,
"Kadacket, kadacket!"
My little red hen.

And so I know it's morning
And time to shake a leg.
For my little hen's already
Laid her first plump egg.

BIRDS IN A GARDEN

Yes, my garden's a wee bit wild,
For so the cedar-birds like it, child –
The paths unraked and the lawns unmowed,
The vines unstaked and the weeds unhoed.
But just look there in the berry bush
Where the cedar-birds feed and a hermit thrush,
Where the branches tangle the too unwary
And the robins wrangle over a berry –
They like it woodsy and not too trim.
They like it this way – and I like them.

I WONDER

I wonder as I wander
Along a wooden path
Why a bird
Should pick a puddle
full of mud
to take a bath!

I wonder as I wander
Along a garden lane
Why snails should make
such long long trips
and just go back again

WHO'S THAT CHIRPING?

Who's that chirping, out of sight,
Cheerful chirping in delight?

– Insect in the thicket hid,
Are you cricket? katydid?

I look and look, I listen, listen,
See but leaves and twigs a-glisten.

I'll kneel a minute on the ground.
– No, that scares him. Not a sound.

"Click-it! Click-it!" loud and clear!
He's right beside my listening ear!

Look! – Beneath a leaf – himself!
A tiny green and winged elf!

THE BROOK

The brook runs a-chattering
Over the rocks,
A-seeking to waken
The sleepy sheep-flocks.

Unheading they slumber,
All humped there a-doze,
Unhearing, uncaring,
While onward she goes.

But she all undaunted
Just ripples along,
Unwearying, singing
Her murmuring song.

HOMES

Earth mother in her love for all
Provides her creatures, large and small,
With homes to fit each shape and size,
Protecting them in wondrous wise.

The birds she teaches how to build
Their nests, with ferns and feathers filled,
Where leafy boughs their secret keep
And breezes rock their young to sleep.

The lion sleeps along a limb –
No fear of prowling beast for him.
The bear retires to a cave,
The sea-gull to an ocean wave.

A webby home the spider weaves,
Both bed and supper there she finds.
Cocoon of silk among the leaves
A caterpillar deftly winds.

The lowly mole digs him a hole,
The eagle builds an eyrie high.
To one the dark warm earth is dear,
The other loves the lonely sky.

The cowrie in his curven shell
Is washed, unworried by the waves,
Along the pebbly shore, where dwell
The sea anemone in their caves.

The turtle wears a shell well planned,
A moving house, to ward off harm,
Then trusting, lays her eggs in sand
For sun and earth themselves to warm.

Their storied chambers in the dirt
From grain on grain, ants careful build,
To keep their eggs and young from hurt,
From hungry foes or getting chilled.

The bees build honeyed halls of wax
Within their hive, and there they dwell,
In sunny harmony their tasks fulfill
And eat and sleep as well.

Beneath the earth the rabbit hides,
Beneath the sea the awesome whale.
In own abode each one abides,
It may be small or giant-scale.

But man his kind of home may choose
And build it how or where he will,
A cabin or a castle for his use,
For God a shining temple on a hill.

SAILING

There was an aged lady,
There was an aged man,
They bought an aged sailboat
To sail where sailors can.

She snuffed a pinch of pepper,
He sniffed a pinch of snuff,
    Then both did sneeze
    And made a breeze
That blew them far enough.

SIR CAT

In the market, lights are out.
Hungry mouse tiptoes about,
Peeks discreetly 'round a corner.
Oops! Sir Cat is almost on her!

Mouse runs headlong past the cheeses,
Finds spilled pepper – rashly sneezes.
– Soon, Sir Cat returns, but proudly,
Licks his whiskers, purring loudly.

I NEVER MET A LION

I never met a lion.
    I never hope to meet one.
But if I ever do one day,
    I know just how I'd greet one.

I'd bow and say politely,
    "I hope you're in good health, sir,"
And, "If you'll let me go my way,
    I'll give you all my wealth, sir."

Then I'd empty out my pockets
    Of things I keep there just for fun,
And while he was a-sorting them,
    I'd run and run and run!

DUST DEVIL

Folk call me Dust Devil,
but little they know –
Neither where I have come from,
nor whither I go.

I'm really a whirlwind,
although I'm so small,
I whirl dust around me
to make myself tall.

Sometimes I am fat,
sometimes I am thin,
as faster and faster
I whirl and I spin.

(read faster and faster)

It may make you dizzy
to follow my dance,
as over the bush-tops
I leap and I prance.

Watch out, or I'll catch you
and wrap you about
in a furious dust-cloud!

(pause)

and then let you out.

– Then off to the desert
I'll frolic away,
blowing dust round the sages
the rest of the day.

THINGUMABOBS

"Oh Mother, first my thingummy broke,
And now it's my hickey-ma-do!
I haven't a single toy that works,
And it's rainy outdoors, too!"

"I'll have to go to the hodge-podge drawer
And get you a thingumajig.
Then you can mend your hickey-ma-do
With a string and a bit of twig."

" Oh, Mother always thinks of something
For troubles, small or big.
She'll tie my laces, bandage knees,
And help me mend my thingumajig."

RIDDLE

As red as a heart,
As round as a rose –
If you squeeze me too hard
I'll drip on your clothes.

As smooth as a cheek,
As soft as a lip –
I'm delicious to eat
And mighty good to sip.

(A tomato)

RIDDLE

Its home is a hole
And it has a brown skin,
But it isn't a mole
And it's white within.

It's rather small-size,
But it's round and it's fat.
It sometimes has eyes,
But it's blind as a bat.

People boil it or bake it
Or steam it or fry it,
But they won't let you take it
If the doctor says to diet.

(A potato)

ALLITERATIONS

Twenty swarthy worthy dwarves,
Swiftly snitched some twisted twigs,
Stiffly sniffing twitched their whiskers,
Sipped from snifters twenty swigs.

***

Smugly smiling smelly smokers
Smirk and smear their smudgy smocks.

***

Six whistling thistle-siskins sit,
That whisk and twist 'twixt thistle-twigs.

***

A snake and a snail and a snapping turtle,
Named Sniffle, Snicker and Snoop,
Were snatching a snack in the noonday sun,
Until they began to droop.
"Let us snooze," said Sniffle to Snoop with a sneer.
"Very well," snapped Snoop. "But we can't do it here!"

Whirling, whisking,
Briskly frisking,
Reckless risking
Life and limb.

Twirling trickster,
Twisting, risked her
Whiskery neck
To rescue him.

***

A feminine anemone too late
From out her tenement did emanate.
An imminent enemy anonymous,
Who met her in a manner ominous,
Soon did anemone eliminate.

ROISTER'S LITHP

Roister Doister
Found an oyster,
Cracked it with his teeth.
Now, poor lad, can only thay,
There mutht have been
thome other way.

A LAY ON LYING

Birds and bugs and fish lay eggs.
An impish child may lay a pie
Where someone else will sit on it.
But sleeping dogs don't lay – they lie!

People lie, for rest relieves them.
If otherwise, no one believes them.
Let's have no lying in our words,
And let's leave laying to the birds.

WIGGLER

Toward me he came with lizard slither
And fixed me with his saurian eye.
I care not whence you came, nor why,
Said I,
You hied yourself a-wriggle hither –
And little where you go care I.
   – Just, please sir, wiggle thither.

SPIDERS

I hated as a little child
A spider's web across my face.
But now I've come to recognize
That spiders have their place.

A spider in a sunlit window
Has built her fragile dome,
Invited sun's bright prisms
To decorate our home.

I've made my peace with spiders
At the age of eighty-three.
They're free to build their palaces
And catch the light for me.

BUMBLE BEE

Humble bumble bee a-humming,
Sitting in the summer sun,
Sipping nectar, going, coming
From the clovers every one –
Sometimes on your head you tumble,
Fumble through the weedy way,
But we never hear you grumble,
Though you toil the livelong day.
Visiting the flowers cheery,
All day long you come and go.
Do you never grow a-weary
Busily a-buzzing so?

A RIDE FOR THE BOYS

Rickety, rackety,
lickety, leap.
My brother'll take us
to ride in his jeep.

Up in the morning
at half-past night.
Swallow your breakfast
and then sit tight.

Crackety, clackety,
limpety, lurch,
past the minister,
past the church.

Chiggety, chuggety,
jerkety, squirt.
Hit the highway,
hit the dirt.

Faster! Faster!
Pour it on, man!
Drive it faster
if you can!

Rattlety, clattery,
crashety, - Bang!
– He swung to the left
when he should of swang.

But there's no sense cryin'
when the milk is spilled.
We're just darn lucky
we didn't get killed.

A WINDY NIGHT IN SPACE

One walloping wintery windy night
When the stars were clear and the moon was bright,
Paul said to Wolf, and Wolf said to Will,
"Tonight is the night. Let's go to the hill."

First they went to the barn where their secret lay,
The Thing they had talked of night and day –
The Thing they had made with their own bare hands,
The Thing that would take them to far-off lands.

They went at once to the empty stall
Where they had hidden It, string and all.
They gathered It up. Then they grinned and said,
"What do you bet, this'll sure beat bed!"

They tugged and they lugged to the top of the hill.
"You get in first," said Wolf to Will.
"A wind like this will carry all three –
We'll just tie the string to the top of the tree."

It rattled a bit as the boys climbed in,
And the wind picked it up with a furious din.
"We're off!" cried the boys, and they held their ears.
"We always said it would fly! Three cheers!"

The wind blew harder, with might and main.
"Do you think," asked Wolf, "it'll take us to Spain?"
"What country," cried Paul, "is that below?
It sure doesn't look like any I know."

Will answered only, "The stars are so bright!"
"You've never been up in the sky at night,"
Said the others. But it still got brighter.
Will spoke again. "You've never been righter."

The Old Moon opened her big yellow eye.
"What's this that's coming so close to my sky?
It looks, for the world, like a big box kite
With three boys inside. How could that be right?"

"Hey it's the Moon!" "The Moon? So soon?"
"I don't see a man, but it sure is the Moon!"
"I say, this'll make the early show!"
"They'd never believe it, down below."

"Hey fellows, look! She's getting away!"
"Moon, Moon, wait! Please stay! Please stay!"
A distant voice said, "I never wait.
The world would stop, were I to be late."

"Hey, fellows, we're standing still!" cried Paul.
"We've come to the end of our string, that's all."
And down the sky the old Moon slid,
And left the boys there, she did, she did.

———————————————

TOBIAS

Tobias, son of Tobit, son of Tobiel,
Grew up a lad who loved his father well.
It grieved his heart to see his father blind,
Who was to others generous and kind.

He prayed for help to make his father well,
And God did send him Angel Raphael.
The same did guide him on a journey long
That ended in Tobias' wedding song.

When he returned, not only did he bring
A bride to make his happy parents sing,
But a healing remedy as well
That made his father see, through Raphael.

SAINT MICHAEL
or
TOWARD BROTHERHOOD

There is a dragon lives near me,
Who often bids me do what's wrong.
But I don't listen to his plea,
Boldly I sing a different song.

I sing: O Angel, be my guide.
Lead me to Saint Michael.
Straight will I walk with him beside
And bid him in my heart to dwell.

Saint Michael, lend me your sword,
Make me strong for doing good.
Kind be my deeds and pure my words,
My heart be filled with brotherhood.

THE SILENT GOD, VIDAR

Gone is the Sun from the sky,
Where Sol so long drove it in glory.
Gone are the gods from on high.
Gone is great Odin, who moved in the wind and the weather,
Silent the thundering hammer of Thor.
Done are the deeds of the gods and forgotten.
No man may remember them more.
Dayless, the world sleeps in darkness.
Moonless, the night broods with gloom.
Fenrer, the greedy one, prowls in his hunger.
Ragnarok rules in the dark and the doom.

But Ragnarok's nights may be numbered.
Thor is dead; but the heartbeat of man goes on.
And deep in the heart, the memory slumbers
Of the promise of Vidar, the Silent One.
For the Vala told Odin of *this* son the future –
How in time a New Day would be born,
When Vidar the valiant would rise and avenge him,
His voice, so long silent, the Wolf overcome.
Then a new race of gods will arise altogether,
To dwell in the halls of the old ones long dead.
Then will Baldur in beauty the Earth again brighten,
A carpet of flowers spring up at his tread.
'Tis Vidar the veils of the mist will withdraw then,
So that now sons of men with new light in their eyes
May look up to the heavens unclouded.
Reborn, a new Sun will glow bright in the skies,
And aloft bear the daughter of Sol in full glory.

THE EAGLE

Long, long ago, you, Eagle, lord
Above lost continents have soared.
In lonely vigil till man came
To light on Earth his little flame.
You watched his golden cities rise,
His altar fires climb the skies.
You watched the heroes fall in wars
On ancient long-forgotten shores.

Now still you love the lonely height,
Before day dawns on Earth, delight
In being first to see the sun –
And last again, when day is done.
Through sunlit hours you soar on high,
A king of air and azure sky,
And then at eve you seek your rest
On craggy peak in wind-blown nest.

My thoughts, like you, would swiftly soar
Over the world of air and shore,
Would feel Sun's power filling them,
As far and wide they range and skim,
Seeking their goals in tireless quest –
Then turning home for sleep and rest.

LIKE AND LIKE

A small flower-bell
Out of earth's dark gloom
Had sprouted up early
Into delicate bloom.

Along came a bee
And sipped of her dew –
They seem to be made
For each other, these two.

– Goethe
Translated by BDB

(Quoted in an article on teaching botany,
especially insect relationships, in *Das Goetheanum*
54: 43: 340.)

ARTIST SPRING

Artist Spring,
Errant thing,
Splashes her canvas
With lyrical swing.

Daubing the hilltops
A mustard bold,
She eloquent follows
With poppies' pure gold.

Dipping her brushes
In lupine blue,
She fills every hollow
With more than its due.

Then over the valleys
As sign she has been,
She empties her pots
With intemperate fling.

RUFOUS

His gorget flashing fire as he flies,
a flame of humming bird arrives
from outer skies.
His golden target, aloes,
know his coming
and tremble with surmise.

For him no artful ruses,
for them no place to hide.
He lifts imperious bill
and quintessential juices
from every aloe trumpet
pour inside.

A score and more of flowers
he delicately ravishes,
and sans excuse for seeming rude
he fire-filled and fire-fed
swings wide
and powers toward infinitude.

WINTER DREAMS

Let us step softly
   over the earth,
For seeds lie asleep there
   awaiting new birth.

One little seed
   in the garden bed
Is Magnolia's child
   in her nightgown of red.

She dreams of a flower
   that lived long ago –
A magnolia flower
   with petals like snow.

She dreams of the autumn –
   how things used to be
In the cone with her brothers
   way up in the tree.

The day the cone opened
   on its bough up so high,
Both she and her brothers
   first saw the wide sky.

Then a rough wind blew
   and it shook the cone,
And she tumbled down
   to the ground, alone.

She fell in brown leaves
   and slid out of sight.
And so had begun
   her long long night.

A gnome came and pushed her
   down into the ground
And told her to lie there
   and not make a sound.

So cold it was there,
   so dark and so dreary,
She soon fell asleep,
   though she wasn't that weary.

Was it an angel,
   or did it just seem so,
Who leaned down to bring her
   a golden bright dream?

In her dream three planets
   were riding on high,
And she watched as they wove there
   a trail through the sky.

"Some day they will call you,"
   the angel said.
"But until that day comes,
   you must rest in your bed."

So she rested and slept,
   as she had been told,
Until a day came
   when it seemed less cold.

She waked up and stretched –
   or tried so to do.
Her shell was quite wet,
   but she couldn't break through.

It seemed she would burst
   with the longing inside her.
"Won't someone please help me?"
   in a small voice she cried.

Did she feel a slight movement
   in the earth below?
There was an opening
   and she stuck out a toe.

A wonderful warmth
   flowed down from above,
And she thrust up her arms
   in a rush of love.

– There it was at long last –
   the gold light of the Sun!
The victory over
   the darkness was won!

THUNDERSTORM

Shout the wild huzzas!
Crack the mighty whips!
The wrothy gods from heaven lean,
With demons come to grips!

Let down your torrents! Wash out woe!
Split the cloudy heavens wide!
One fleeting moment only show
The gleaming light inside.

I NEED SOMEONE

I need someone
Who stands taller than I.

And you need someone
Who stands taller than you.

If we hold hands
And stand on tip toe,
Will that do?

ACORN

Not by the thunder
The boulder was riven
That lies there asunder,
Helplessly cloven.

Not any mortal,
Of chisel though master,
Marked this for portal
Nor chose for pilaster.

Not any giant,
For gold or for gain,
Maimed the defiant
And clove it in twain.

Might, them denied,
To an acorn was given,
To spring the stone wide
And thrust upward to heaven

AUTUMN LEAVES

"Where did the colors go, O mother,
The oranges and the reds, that glowed
So brightly on the branches
Only a moment ago?

The leaves I kick along the ground,
These leaves are brown that swirl around –
Surely they were orange and red
Not long ago. – Now – are they dead?"

"The leaves are dead, but their colors live on –
So the poets say – in your heart and mine.
There they will glow like the golden sun
And from our hearts forever shine."

CANDLE IN THE WIND

A spark, a flame, a raging fire
devours the mountainside,
fed by a wildly racing wind,
insatiable, demoniac.
Flames leap from ridge to ridge,
firs fall, the mightiest cedars crash.
The howling wind moves on
leaving behind but ash.

       – And still, if sheltered by a hand,
       one candle in the wind
       may stand.

SONGS

Songs

Those of us who are fortunate to live and work with young children in the roles of parents and teachers know that to be able to observe their gradual development is a privilege and an opportunity toward self-knowledge. During his/her lifetime on earth each human being recapitulates the evolutionary journey of mankind. This is a journey of becoming an "I," an individual, each with unique endowments. The young child, until the change of teeth, is living in imaginative consciousness, in fantasy. There is as yet no real subjectivity; there is rather an experience of being "one" with the surrounding world.

In order to translate these early experiences into musical language, we have to refer to the intervals as they occur within the tonal scale. In lecture 5 (March 7, 1923) of *The Inner Nature of Music and the Experience of Tone*, Rudolf Steiner describes the journey of each child on earth as a path through the musical intervals: from the "fifth" during early childhood; to the "third" (both major and minor) from the ninth year; and then at twelve years of age, the octave. In our time we speak of the pentatonic scale (experienced linearly) as being the appropriate musical vehicle for the child under nine years of age. What we need to be aware of is that the intervals within the "linear" pentatonic scale are a sequence of seconds and thirds, i.e. d e g a b d'e'. What then do we mean by "mood of the fifth"?

Those of you familiar with musical terms will know the concept of "The Circle of Fifths." Over time the placement of the tones on the circle has changed. I will use the one known to students of music based on Anthroposophy.

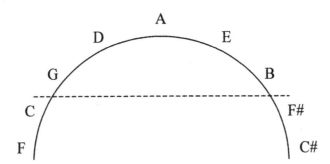

If we give the tone A the uppermost position on the circle, then on the left we have D and on the right we have E. Continuing on either side of D and E, we would come to G on the left and B on the right. We now have the five tones of the "penta" scale in distances of fifths. Many years of tonal research have revealed the "light" and "dark" aspects of these tones, and have established that the B possesses the "lightest" quality.

Let us now consider the tonal path of incarnation of each individual human being. This path would progress from "light" spheres to "denser" spheres, as the incarnational development from the head ("light") to the limbs ("denser"). Musically speaking we now move from B (most light filled) to E, A, D and G (gradual densification). Penetrating still further we then meet C and F. For our consideration we need to understand the process of movement from "fifths" to "scale."

Let us look at the following diagram:

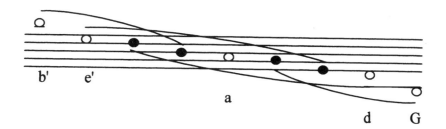

Here we have the five tones (in fifths) on the music staff. The human voice can comfortably span the double fifth from d – a – e' in singing. The linear or melodic pentatonic scale comes about through the transposition of the tones b' and G to the middle octave, where they can be sung without strain, and by repeating the high e' in the lower octave and the low d in the higher octave. We do have to remember, however, the central position of the tone 'a' around which all "mood of the fifth" songs are created.

In this lovely collection, Barbara Betteridge has created songs for the pre-school and first grade- age child, as for example "Busy Bee," "Soon Cometh the Spring," "Elves' Song," and "Far Are the Stars"; for second grade the songs "Gingerbread Man," "Bumble Bee," "Lullaby," and "Evening Song"; and for third grade the songs "Pippa's Song," "On the Mountain," "Song for Saint Martin's," "Glory," "Swing Bell," and "Sandman." These latter songs (third grade) all have a wonderful folksong quality, as from the Celtic or Appalachian heritage.

I conclude this foreword with Barbara Betteridge's own words: "If these songs inspire others who teach music to try working in the 'mood of the fifth' and the pentatonic mode, and eventually to become creative with them themselves, they will have served their purpose."

— Channa Andriesse Seidenberg
Philmont, NY
March 2005

Busy Bee

B D Betteridge

Zum   zum   zum   bus y bee a hum

Fly	a	way	in	sun	ny	wea	ther	to	the	gar	den	to	the	hea	ther
Seek	the	blos	som,	seek	the	flow	er,	don't	get	caught	in	sud	den	show	er.
Ga	ther	nec	tar,	ga	ther	pol	len,	bring	it	home,	see	none	be	fal	len.
Store	a	way	your	gol	den	hon	ey,	rich	er	trea	sure	far	than	mon	ey.
Muf	fins	we	will	have	for	sup	per,	gold	en	hon	ey,	gold	en	but	ter.

Zum   zum   zum   bus — y bee a hum.

Soon Cometh the Spring

B D Betteridge
C Morgenstern

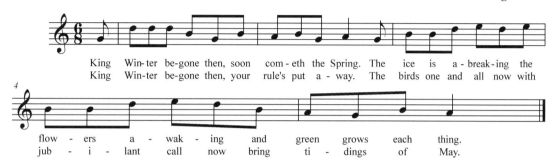

King Win-ter be-gone then, soon com-eth the Spring. The ice is a - break-ing the
King Win-ter be-gone then, your rule's put a - way. The birds one and all now with

flow - ers a - wak - ing and green grows each thing.
jub - i - lant call now bring ti - dings of May.

Elves' Song

B D Betteridge
J W Goethe

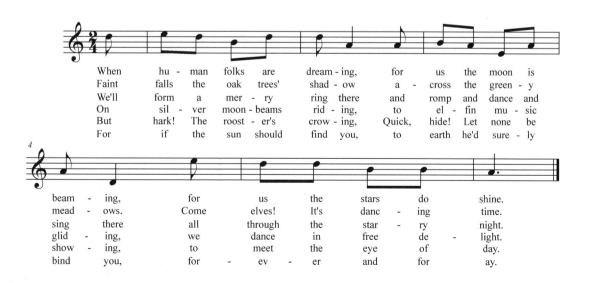

When hu - man folks are dream - ing, for us the moon is
Faint falls the oak trees' shad - ow a - cross the green - y
We'll form a mer - ry ring there and romp and dance and
On sil - ver moon - beams rid - ing, to el - fin mu - sic
But hark! The roost - er's crow - ing, Quick, hide! Let none be
For if the sun should find you, to earth he'd sure - ly

beam - ing, for us the stars do shine.
mead - ows. Come elves! It's danc - ing time.
sing there all through the star - ry night.
glid - ing, we dance in free de - light.
show - ing, to meet the eye of day.
bind you, for - ev - er and for ay.

33

Far Are the Stars

B D Betteridge

Far are the stars _____ glow-ing so gold - ly
Fol - low them far _____ fol - low them bold - ly
Hark how all hea - ven rings an - gels with gold - en wings sing-ing a - far.

Gingerbread Man

B D Betteridge

Gin- ger bread, gin-ger bread, gin-ger bread man. Stir him up and roll him out and
pat him in the pan! A rai - sin for a nose. In the
o - ven now he goes. Gin - ger bread, gin - ger bread, gin - ger bread man.
Bake him now and take him out as quick as ev - er you can.

Bumble Bee

B D Betteridge

Hum-ble bum-ble bee a hum-ming sit-ting in the sum-mer sun Sip-ping nec-tar go-ing com-ing

from the clo-vers ev-'ry one. Some-times on your head you tum-ble fum-ble through the weed-y way,

But we ne-ver hear you grum-ble tho' you toil the live-long day. Vis-it-ing the flow-ers chee-ry

all day long you come and go Do you ne-ver grow a-wear-y bus-i-ly a buz-ing so?

Lullaby

B D Betteridge

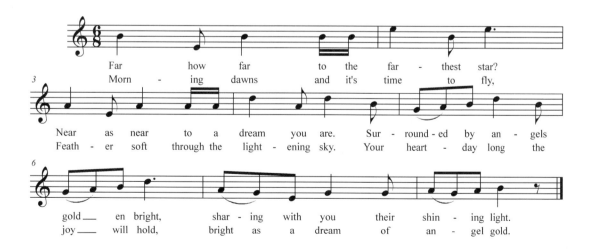

Far   how   far   to   the   far - thest   star?
Morn — ing   dawns   and   it's   time   to   fly,

Near   as   near   to   a   dream   you   are.   Sur - round-ed   by   an - gels
Feath - er   soft   through the   light - ening sky.   Your   heart - day long   the

gold __ en bright,   shar - ing   with   you   their   shin - ing light.
joy __ will hold,   bright   as   a   dream   of   an - gel gold.

35

Evening Song

B D Betteridge

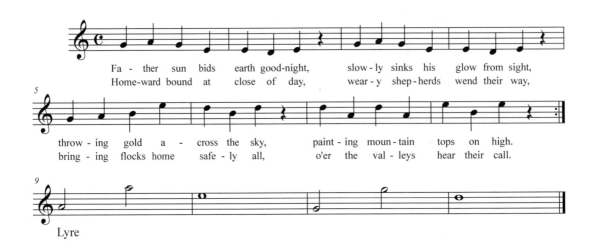

Fa - ther sun bids earth good-night, slow - ly sinks his glow from sight,
Home-ward bound at close of day, wear - y shep - herds wend their way,

throw - ing gold a - cross the sky, paint - ing moun - tain tops on high.
bring - ing flocks home safe - ly all, o'er the val - leys hear their call.

Lyre

Pippa's Song

B D Betteridge
R Browning

The year's at the Spring. The day's at the morn.

Morn- ing's at sev - en, the hill - side's dew pearled. The lark's on the wing. The

snail's on the thorn. God's in His hea - ven all's right with the world.

On The Mountain

B D Betteridge
La Motta

Song for Saint Martin's

B D Betteridge
after M Tittmann

Glory

B D Betteridge

Have   you   heard   the   an - gels   sing   Glo - o - ry.
All   night   long   the   hea - vens   ring

Now   by   day   our   voi - ces   ring   Glo - o - ry.
For   we   all   so   love   to   sing

Shep - herds   call - ing   in   the   hills   Hal - loo - oo.
How   their   call   the   val - ley   fills

Hark!   One   ans - wers   far   a - way   Hal - loo - oo.
Wan - d'ring   home   at   close   of   day

Swing Bell

B D Betteridge

A snow - flake fell and lit on a bell, oh
The snow flake fell up - on___ the bell, oh
And when the bell had rung___ full well, snow

bell a - ring, oh bell a - swing, a -
bell a - ring, oh both a - swing, a
flake was gone, so ends my song, a

long, a - long. Ding dong, ding dong.
long, a long. Ding dong, ding dong.
long, a long. Ding dong, ding dong.

Sandman

B D Betteridge

The lambs have left their leap - ing, come sand - man strew your sand. The blos - soms all are sleep - ing through - out the si - lent land. On - ly the an - gels watch are keep-ing. Sleep, oh sleep, my child - ren.

PLAYS

CLASS PLAYS IN WALDORF SCHOOLS

"All the world's a stage," and children sense it almost from year one. The youngest show-off is play-acting, hoping to get attention as the prettiest or the smartest child – or even as the roughest and rudest, whichever ideal is called forth by the environment at the moment.

For the ideal is ever the stuff of play-acting – the ideal which is more real than what we call reality. In his soul the young child tries to get a better hold on so-called reality by turning the outer real into fantasy. In his play he acts out his hopes and fears, his joys and frustrations, thereby revealing himself to others, and at the same time seeking balance, healing. Teachers and therapists and many parents have observed this.

If it seems sometimes that in a Waldorf school "the play's the thing," from nursery school all the way up, parents have no need to worry that the three R's are giving way to mere frills.

Take kindergarten, for example. Fairy tales provide the main substance here, and "dress-up day," when the children in their turn become kings and queens, sorcerers and witches, is not only the most looked forward to day of the week, it is quite possibly the most educational. For to experience inwardly and act out both good and evil, to be one week a queen and the next a witch, without being punished in the ordinary sense for one's bad behavior, or perhaps embarrassed about one's good behavior, lets children sample the stuff of life in both their feeling and their experience. A child discovers for himself that he has a better feeling about himself when he is striving to be kingly than when he is acting the wicked sorcerer. Can anyone think of a better preparation for facing the dangers and temptations that will come in adolescence than such an innocent, experimental moving between the realms of good and evil in the early years and the resulting feelings and impulses that may form a lasting link with the moral element, out of the child's innate preference?

This way, surely, lies a reality more persuasive than the harshest scolding or the most inventive sermon. And this kind of reality is at work in many plays also beyond the fairy tale level.

How plays are used from grades one to eight depends in a Waldorf school on the individual teacher who guides the class through all eight years. Fortunately few teachers ever emphasize plays as performances, as entertaining an audience or showing how remarkable the children are, much less as preparation for possible careers on the stage. The emphasis lies rather on plays as useful tools in the process of educating, of awakening the children inwardly and bringing them to life.

The wealth plays have to contribute as such tools would take many pages to proclaim. On the practical level, a child who finds reading difficult will really make an effort to read his or her part in a play. Why? Because a play is – well, *play*. We all recognize that a child whose interest is aroused performs better on every level. For the same reason, a play that is built around the main lesson – be it the Old Testament, Norse mythology, the Trojan War or mineralogy – such a play enhances the learning experience connected with that block. The content comes to life, while the repetition involved in play rehearsals makes it stick. At the same time the literary quality of the language, if the plays used are well written, helps to develop good taste and balance of soul. Social development and personal interrelating are also enhanced. Poise, quick wittedness (we think of the child whose crown falls off and who ad-libs a line without missing a beat), the ability to speak well – all these are obvious outgrowths of the work in dramatics. Even the child who really prefers to paint scenery, sew costumes or operate the lights can find in dramatics a sphere of excellence. All the world's a stage, and there is room for both players and stage hands.

– Barbara Betteridge
February 1983

MONT SAINT MICHEL

by Barbara Betteridge
After a Norman legend

CAST

ST. MICHAEL
CHOIR OF ANGELS
FIVE FISHERMEN: PIERRE, OLD JACQUES, JEAN, ANTOINE, FRANÇOIS
SATAN
LITTLE DEVILS: RIX, RAX, TRICK, TRACK, SNICK, SNACK, SNOCK,
                  PREX, KEX, ROKE, NOKE

SCENE I

[*The company enters singing, or reciting.*]

COMPANY: In far-off France, in Normandy,
There lies a mountain by the sea.
When tides roll in, this rocky cone
Amidst the water stands alone.
But when the tides roll out again,
The sheep may wander on the plain.
And on this rock there proudly stand
Fortress, church and castle grand.
Who made the hill and castle? Tell!
Once Satan fought with Mi-cha-el.
He was by Michael overcome
And in a trade, he suffered some.
Since then he's never had his way.
Now, quiet be and mark our play,

SATAN: [*Squats on stone block and peers out, while two little devils tussle over his scepter.*]
Right icy, winter days are these,
When stone and bone could easy freeze.
Your work, Friend Frost, you've done quite right –
I must enjoy your chilly might.
[*To the little devils*]
See here, you devils, knaves, take care!

You'll likely smash my scepter, there!
But rather, tell me, who goes yonder?
Is't not my neighbor lord, I wonder?
Of heaven's host, the proudest prince?
(Just such a one was I, long since.)

RIX: Sir Satan, you've not guessed amiss,
                  Strong Michael indeed it is.

RAX: He seems quite often here to come.

SATAN: You fools, leave off your chatter dumb!
                  You call him strong? Mere spirit, he!
                  The Ruler of the Earth *I* be!
                  But watch you, while a trick I play.
                  [*To Michael*]
                  Ho there, you Prince of Heaven, what say?
                  What do you find it really worth,
                  My rocky realm of ice and earth?
                  Hark how it racks and crackles here!
                  Unlimited my power, 'tis clear!

MICHAEL: O Satan, with your sport have done!
                  Almighty, there is only One.

ANGEL CHOIR: [*Tune: Doxology. Sing two lines, perhaps hum the rest, or* "Vom Himmel
        Hoch"]
                  God is almighty, He alone.
                  In Earth and Heaven, only one.

SATAN: [*Holding his ears*]
                  What plagues my ears with din so dire?
                  I spoke to you and not a choir!
                  You Spirit, empty words you love.
                  A *word* is easy, 'tis *deeds* that prove.
                  I challenge you this very hour
                  To try your fortune with God's power.
                  With power my *own*, to you I'll show
                  That *I'm* the master here below.

MICHAEL: [*Quietly but forcefully*]
                  I'm ready, but the deed you'll rue.

SATAN: You build a castle, I'll build one too.

One night we'll have, both you and me.
Then which is better, we shall see.

RIX AND RAX: It will be ours. Hee! Hee! Hee! Hee!
We'll help you, Master, willingly!

SATAN: [*To Michael*]

Do you accept this challenge strange?

MICHAEL: [*Already distant*]

What I have said, I do not change.

SATAN: [*To the tussling Devils*]

He's not so talkative today
Now, Rix and Rax, leave off your play!
Fetch here the devil's demon pack –
First, Trick and Track, Snick, Snock and Snack.
Then Prex and Kex, then Roke and Noke –
The whole array of devil folk.
Bring every knave here right away,
Before the sunlight fades today.

[*Rix and Rax rush, screeching, away.*]

SCENE II

[*Satan directs the little Devils, who are approaching, laden with stones.*]

SATAN: Just throw them on the heap. Keep on!
Don't stop for breath until it's done!

TRICK: It's high already! See, the rocks
Look like a tower of giant blocks!

TRACK: From farthest corners of the land,
Yon granite blocks have come to stand.

SNICK: My, that will be a castle grand!

SATAN: Don't jabber so! Hark my command:
Bring rock, in SLABS! Bring chunks galore!
[*Striking at the nearest one*]
Fly off and fetch it fast! Still more!

SNOCK: [*With some long stones*]
>
> These are for pillar, post and pier.

SATAN:
>
> Just throw them down. [*To the others*] You there! See here!
> Put lots of rubble in between,
> For cracks and joints must not be seen.

SNACK: [*With very little rock*]
>
> We only found a little more.

SATAN:
>
> Then dig it from the rocky shore.
> The coast has quite enough of cliffs
> To trap like rats the pretty ships,
> Where we've oft lured them unaware.
> See yonder rocky ledges there –
> Some jagged crags are next in need,
> Your claws can break them off with speed.
> For decoration we require –
> Like turrets – and perhaps a spire.
> [*While more stones are being brought, Satan goes aside and rubs his paws.*]
> Hear them shatter! Hear them smashing!
> What a clatter! What a crashing!
> Hear the thunder roll and row!
> [*Listens*]
> But what is my neighbor doing now?
> There's not a sound from over yonder.
> What is *he* up to, I wonder.

SNACK:
>
> He's hunting him some spirits still –
> Some angels, elves, or what you will.

SATAN: [*With a mocking laugh*]
>
> His buildings can't be heard or seen!
> He builds with light and air, I ween –
> And not like me, with solid earth.
> [*Sneeringly*]
> A castle of air! What is that worth?
> [*He laughs over his joke.*]

ANGEL CHOIR:
>
> What God has made, do not despise.
> By light of day, 'twill meet your eyes.

SCENE III

[Satan squats in his circle of Devils.]

SATAN:

Look sharp, for almost gone is night.
Soon will my castle greet the light.
[He gives a chunk of stone one more shove.]
This block of stone is not yet righted –
Here's how it goes! Now, I'm delighted!
What more could anyone desire?
Come, devils, knaves, my work admire!

DEVILS: *[All together]*

Spectacular! Colossal, ay!
Your castle grandly greets the day!

SATAN:

Does it not make a pompous show?

DEVILS:

None but a master can build *so*!
The victory's yours, there's no denying!
St. Michael soon will come a-crying!

ANGEL CHOIR: *[Turning quietly toward the other side]*

How light and clear the towers rise,
In curving arches, climb the skies!
The shafted columns, proud and free,
Rise, too, in solemn majesty.
Like thousand crystal's glance and glimmer,
Transparent as a glacier's shimmer,
The vaulted walls and mighty halls,
The spires and the capitals!

SATAN: *[Who assumes they are speaking of his building]*

Bravo! And so you must admit,
My work is wondrous, every bit.
'Twas mine the power, mine the art.
In this, no other had a part.

DEVILS:

As no one ever would have guessed,
You've won the wager. Yours is best.

SATAN: *[To the Choir]*

It's well that you agree, at that.
But hold! What are you gawking at?
My castle stands behind all you.
Pray, is there something else to view?

49

ANGEL CHOIR: Thou fool! The beauteous one lies there.
(To turn around he does not dare.)

SATAN: Why should I then at nothing stare?
What's there to see in empty air?

MICHAEL: [*Calmly and grandly*]
Turn thee, and let thine eye behold
What help from God did there unfold.

SATAN: [*Turns about angrily and stands as though enchanted*]

DEVILS: [*Who have also turned and are terrified*]
Ow! How it blind our eyes with pain!
[*Turn back*]
Quick! Turn around again!

ANGEL CHOIR: [*To Satan*]
And now, pray tell, how do you feel?

SATAN: [*Slowly*]   I'm fooled! The beauty is not real!
Unreal! The castle's only seeming!
Must be mirage – or else I'm dreaming!
[*Feels his eyes*]
My eyes are wide! I'm not asleep.
Quickly devils, through this mist do leap!

SEVERAL DEVILS: [*Holding their eyes shut, jump and are bumped*]
Ow me! My head! Don't jump again!

SATAN: It must be solid substance then.
[*Grimly*] I've lost, and must digest my sorrow.
Pray, Michael, meet me here tomorrow.

MICHAEL: Once more I'll come and then I'm done.

SATAN: Right here, at dawn's first rays of sun.
[*Departs*]

DEVILS: We are not ready yet to mourn.
Somehow the sheep will yet be shorn.

ANGEL CHOIR: The beauteous sight bold Satan saw –
Could only stand and gape with awe.
High spirits' help he may not claim,

Who here as *Michael's* helpers came:
Star forces in snow crystals lying
Form force that chill's the water's flying.
Spirits of light, from inward raying,
Bright colors in the world displaying.

SCENE IV

[*Satan appears and regards Michael's castle.*]

SATAN:
There stands the castle. I haven't dreamed it.
Oh night of torment! Sleepless seemed it.
I felt me sick in every bone,
As I this wonder thought upon,
Belonging to the man of heaven –
For *I* may not *possess* it even!
[*Making appropriate gestures*]
Yet ever did I sit and ponder:
Can I gain it still, I wonder?
How envy gnawed the flesh of me!
[*Ponders*] How were it if I'd pious be?

ANGEL CHOIR:
Should Michael trust thy piety?
Deep in thy heart he's bound to see.

DEVILS:
He'll not suspect it is a lie.
Goodhearted *he*. 'Tis *we* are sly.

SATAN. [*To the Devils*]
He comes! Make haste! Get set to yowl!
Now, devils, knaves! Begin to howl!

[*They howl piteously. Michael wants to speak. Satan says, "Sh! Sh!" to the little Devils. When it grows quiet, Michael speaks.*]

MICHAEL:
I promised you might speak again.
But can your word be honored then?

SATAN:
Not always so, I must confess.
That's why my babes are in distress.
In all my pain they take a part.
I wish I had an honest heart.
But evil ever mixes in.
I would be good – it comes between.

But in this night that was so long
I've found a way to right this wrong:
Thy castle is pure light, forsooth.
It tolerates but Good and Truth.
If *I* within this castle dwelt,
Then evil from my heart would melt.
Let us trade off, without ado.
Yours goes to me, and mine to you.

MICHAEL:

My work doth stir your envy still?
I give it you, if that's your will.

[*Satan laughs behind his hand. The little Devils spin around, hopping up and down in glee.*]

ANGEL CHOIR:

Oh, who would grant this bold request!
The end must with the future rest.

SCENE V

ANGEL CHOIR:

From heaps of rubble Satan and his crew
Piled up, a devilish castle grew.
Then spirit hands all this arrayed.
The rocky cone in order laid.
With water girt, it crowns the strand
The water ebbs, and it's on land.
Come fishers, to the heights now wend you
And pray the sea no sorrow send you.
You know, St. Michael is one
Who many a helpful deed has done.

PIERRE:

Today's a catch-day. The wind blows warm.

OLD JACQUES:

Before you leave, 'twould do no harm
To climb the top of yonder hill
And pray that luck your baskets fill.
Then when your boat comes back from sea,
St. Michael thank for guarding thee.

JEAN:

Hast seen the enchanted castle, though
That shines and lures and glitters so?
But woe betide approaching skiffs –
They'd dash to bits on those dread cliffs!

ANTOINE: It is a castle made of ice.
                  A dream could hardly be so nice.
                  Yet who's its owner? I've seen him grin.

FRANÇOIS: It shines as't had sun's fire within.
                  But someone hailed me once from there
                  Who any honest man would scare.

PIERRE: A monster 'tis – a specter vicious!

ANTOINE: [*Looking terrified*]
                  Ho, here he comes! He looks malicious!

FRANÇOIS: The Evil One in dreadful wrath.
                  Oh, hideous voice! Let's clear his path!
                  [*They flee.*]

SATAN: O cursed castle! Now all is lost!
                  The whole night long it pitched and tossed!
                  It dipped and leapt and slipped and quivered!
                  It even melted while I shivered!
                  I couldn't hold nor wood, nor stone.
                  No door it has. No table lone.
                  And everything went slipping, sliding,
                  Or dripping, 'neath the water gliding.
                  It plunged within a whirling pool,
                  My castle proud, left me a fool –
                  Yet never did I touch the ground.
                  Had I not wings, I should have drowned!

MICHAEL: [*To the fishermen*]
                  Come back again, for Satan's fled.
                  Henceforth of him needst have no dread.
                  Come all, and put your trust in me.
                  The Tempter shall not frighten ye.
                  But soon a fortress here shall rise –
                  A castle, church, will meet the skies –
                  Like what you saw, but builded well.

FISHERMEN: It shall be called: Mont Saint Michel!

[*All sing, or recite, the processional with a different closing line.*]

COMPANY:
In far-off France, in Normandy,
There lies a mountain by the sea.
When tides roll in, this rocky cone
Amidst the water stands alone.
But when the tide rolls out again,
The sheep may wander on the plain.
And on this rock there proudly stand
Fortress, church and castle grand.
Who made the hill and castle? Tell!
Once Satan fought with Mi-cha-el.
He was by Michael overcome
And in a trade, he suffered some.
Since then he's never had his way.
Make sure he doesn't, still today!

CURTAIN

OUR FAVORITE STAR

A Play for the Third Grade
By Barbara Betteridge

REMARKS TO THE TEACHER

A play, rightly written, should introduce itself to the audience with *no prior explanations* necessary. In the case of a play for small children, it should introduce itself also to those who are to perform it. If it has to be explained by the teacher beforehand, the artistic effect, the enjoyment will be diminished. It should be fun for them to figure out what the pictures in the play are all about. Sometimes this may come into words ("That means the fishes!"). Sometimes there will just be a secret inner awareness, a realization that the play is really about incarnating human souls, though they are called "Little Angels." It would really spoil the artistic effect for the teacher to put this into words!

Written purposely in fairly simple words, the play is intended to serve also as reading material. After the children have it to some extent by ear, they could have it put into their hands to read. The adult should not be disturbed by cliché phrases or rhymes. There is an age when these experiences are new, are discoveries, and to this age they should be given.

When it comes to dividing the play into parts for individual children, the teacher should take into account that there are four couplets in scene two intended for four different temperaments. A dash at the beginning of a line indicates that a change of speaker is in order, although if it is better suited to the teacher's purposes, much of the material can be recited in chorus.

– Barbara Betteridge
October 1966

OUR FAVORITE STAR

CAST

THREE BIG ANGELS
MANY LITTLE ANGELS

PROLOGUE

[*As the curtain opens, the Little Angels are dancing in Heaven. When they finish their dance, they begin to speak.*]

LITTLE ANGELS: Where do the Big Angels go all day
When they leave us alone in Heaven to play?
– They go to work, but I don't know where.
– Tomorrow, let's watch where they go. Do you dare?

CURTAIN

SCENE I

[*Tomorrow has come, and the Little Angels are standing still as though listening.*]

LITTLE ANGELS: The sound of their wings has died away.
– Let us look where they're going! What do you say?
[*They run to the window ledge of Heaven and, leaning on it, look down.*]
– Down there through the clouds, something new I see!
– It's big and round and as blue as can be.
– Look! It's covered with water – blue and clear.
With waves that roll from here to here. [*Gesturing*]
– It's all growing brighter – can you see?
– Oh, isn't it shining as shining can be!
– There's a veil around it, soft and high,
With little clouds. – Why it's a sky!
– Oh, look what the water's doing now!
It's high over here, over there it is low.
– I think I see something poking through.
It's dark and looks hard, and it's getting wide.
– It's a *shore* that reaches from side to side!
What the angels are doing is what puzzles me.
– They must be working in all that we see.
– Look out! They are back! – Now what will they say?

[*Big Angels enter from backstage, softly moving their wings.*]

56

1ST BIG ANGEL:	So you watched us going to Earth today.
LITTLE ANGELS:	Tell us, we beg you, where you have been!
2ND BIG ANGEL:	How did you like what you have seen?
LITTLE ANGELS:	Oh, it was lovely – shining and new!
3RD BIG ANGEL:	Yes, it is beautiful. That is true.
A LITTLE ANGEL:	May we go there tomorrow, please, to play?
LITTLE ANGELS:	We'll play in the waves and be good all day!

BIG ANGELS: [*Solemnly*] Not tomorrow. It isn't time.

CURTAIN

SCENE II
[Another day in Heaven. The Little Angels are leaning on the window ledge again.]

LITTLE ANGELS: It's the prettiest star in the firmament!
– The angels love it. That must be why.
– The waters are washing their waves on the shores
Till they gleam as white as the clouds in the sky.
[*Slowly*]
– See, in the water – small things that go,
Swaying and swishing, to and fro.
[*Excitedly*]
– And higher and faster, way up in the sky,
Wee things with feathers that flit and fly!
[*Strongly*]
– Look at those animals charging around,
Trampling the jungle as trees fall to ground!
[*Quietly*]
– I love the mountains, above it all,
Covered with snowbanks, so cool and so tall!
Look! There's a garden like Paradise,
With grass and flowers, with fruit and trees –
– And a couple walking that look like us,
Enjoying the garden and the gentle breeze.
– Here come the Angels! Let's really *beg* them
To let us go down to that lovely place!

57

1ST BIG ANGEL:	We heard you and read your thoughts from afar.
2ND BIG ANGEL:	We're happy you like our favorite star.
SOME LITTLE ANGELS:	Sit here while we fan you! Rest from your climb!
OTHER LITTLE ANGELS:	We could help you tomorrow, if you'd take us along.
BIG ANGELS:	—Not tomorrow. It isn't time.

CURTAIN

SCENE THREE

[*Another day, and the Little Angels are talking in Heaven.*]

LITTLE ANGELS:	The Angels looked troubled when they left today.
	– I've a strange dark feeling.
	– I'm bored with play!
	– I wish they'd let us go down to Earth.
	– Well, we can peek – for what it's worth.
	[*Little Angels run to window ledge again.*]
	– The creatures that swim, the creatures that crawl,
	The creatures that fly – I see them all!
	– It would be such fun to join them there!
	– Remember the garden's happy pair?
	I don't see them anywhere today.
	– I see two people, but it couldn't be they,
	They're both together, hand in hand,
	Just sitting there on the barren ground
	Outside the gate.
	– Outside the gate?!
	They'd better go back. It's getting late.
	There's nothing to eat out there in the sand.
	There's nothing to eat in all that land!
	– The gate is locked. They can't go back!
	What will they do?
ALL TOGETHER:	Alas! Alack!
ONE:	To get their food, they'll have to toil.

ANOTHER:	– But we could help them till the soil!
ALL TOGETHER:	– Yes, we could help them make it bloom – Then they would smile and forget their gloom. We'd be their children, and Earth our home. Let's beg the Angels. – Here they come! Angels, Angels, let us go, Down to the loving Earth below!
BIG ANGELS:	Yes, our little Ones, it is time. Prepare yourselves for the long, long climb!
CHORUS OF LITTLE ANGELS:	[*Singing*] Come, wander down the big rainbow To where on Earth we'll live and grow. The Angels say the time has come To leave our high and heavenly home, Forget what we have seen above And learn on Earth to walk and love, To help our fathers till the soil, Make warm their hearts and light their toil. Oh, brothers, sisters, come, let's go! Beloved Earth calls us below!

CURTAIN

GRAMMAR'S GARDEN

by Barbara Betteridge

CAST (Variable)

GARDENER
GARDENER'S WIFE
BOY
GIRL
PUNCTUATION

PARTS OF SPEECH:
NOUNS   (Blue Daisies with paper aprons)
ADJECTIVES   (Yellow-green Fairies with paint brushes and pots)
VERBS   (Red Birds wearing leotards)
ADVERBS   (Orange Birds)
PREPOSITION   (A reddish purple Elf)
ARTICLE   (Littlest Elf, green)
PRONOUN   (Dark blue Elf)
CONJUNCTION   (A brown Elf)

The curtain opens on a garden. On stage right, a gardener and his wife are working. On stage left, stands a fellow called Punctuation, who always stays in this place. The rest of the garden is occupied by all the parts of speech. The Yellow Fairies (Adjectives) are painting the aprons of the Blue Daisies (Nouns). The Littlest Elf (Article) is holding the apron strings of one Daisy. The Red Birds (Verbs) are leaping and flying and running and darting all over the stage, followed by the Orange Birds (Adverbs). The reddish purple Elf (Preposition) moves about among the Daisies, pointing to them, sometimes touching them. The dark blue Elf (Pronoun) stands sometimes behind, sometimes beside a Daisy.

BOY AND GIRL: [*Enter and look around*]

GARDENER: Welcome to Grammar's Garden!

PUNCTUATION: [*Jumps vertically into the air, claps his hands over his head forming a
                     straight line*]
                     Exclamation Point!

GIRL: What is this place?

PUNCTUATION: [*Makes gesture for question*]
                                Question Mark!

GARDENER'S WIFE: It's a garden you've lived in all your lives.

PUNCTUATION: [*Stamps his right foot; calls out*]
                                Period.

GARDENER: [*Talking to Boy and Girl*]
                                Only, you may have never noticed it around you.

PUNCTUATION: [*Stamps other foot; calls out*]
                                Period!

BOY: Who are the strange birds, and all the flowers and the
                                elves?

PUNCTUATION: [*Making proper gesture*]
                                Question Mark!

GARDENER: They are all your friends, and they live in Grammar's
                                Garden.

PUNCTUATION: [*Again stamping foot*]
                                Period.

GIRL: I don't even know their names!

PUNCTUATION: Exclamation Point!

GARDENER'S WIFE: You can surely guess who *that* busybody is.

BOY: He must be Punctuation.

PUNCTUATION: [*Bows. From now on he is quieter but he makes the appropriate gesture for
                                the speech whenever he thinks of it.*]

GARDENER'S WIFE: Now you've got the right idea.

GIRL: Who are you, you flowers in your pretty hats?

ONE OR TWO BLUE DAISIES: We are nouns. We tell what.

OTHER BLUE DAISY:	We tell who.
ALL BLUE DAISIES:	We are names of things and people. Noah, his ark and the bell in the steeple. [*They all bow gracefully.*]
FIRST YELLOW FAIRY:	I wish you'd hold still. You made me smear your beautiful apron.
SECOND YELLOW FAIRY:	I'm painting golden stars on mine.
GIRL:	I can see you like to dress up the nouns.
BOY: [*To the birds who are flitting about*]	You there! You Red Birds! Stop a minute and tell us your names!
BIRDS:	You'll have to catch us first. [*The children chase the Verbs in and out. One of them is still followed by Adverb.*]
TWO RED BIRDS:	We fly! We run! We race for fun!
TWO OTHER BIRDS:	We jump! We swing! We chirp! We sing!
ORANGE BIRDS: [*Stops and points at the chase*]	In! Out! Round about! Here! There! Everywhere!
BOY:	I've caught one of the flitting fellows!
GIRL:	Here's another. Now you two stand still!
PUNCTUATION:	Exclamation Point! [*The chase stops.*] [*During the next sequence, Punctuation jumps up and down the whole time.*]
GARDENER:	Please, all of you, mind your manners now, and tell our guests what you do.
TWO RED BIRDS:	Pour! Pour! Pour!
ORANGE BIRDS:	On! On! On!

TWO OTHER RED BIRDS:	Is burning! Is burning! Is burning!
ONE OR TWO BLUE DAISIES:	Water! Water! Water!
OTHER BLUE DAISIES:	Scotland! Scotland! Scotland!
GIRL:	They make my head whirl. Whatever are they talking about?
BOY:	I get it! The Blue Daisies told us they were Nouns. The red fellows who like to run and fly about so must be Verbs. Listen.

[*The sequence is repeated.*]

RED BIRDS:	Pour! Pour! Pour!
ORANGE BIRDS:	On! On! On!
OTHER RED BIRDS:	Is burning! Is burning! Is burning!
BLUE DAISIES:	Water! Water! Water!
OTHER BLUE DAISIES:	Scotland! Scotland! Scotland!
GARDENER:	It's up to you to make sense of them.

GARDENER'S WIFE: [*Whispering*] Put them in order.

BOY:	I get it. [*Leads them into order*] Now! [*He directs.*]
FIRST BLUE DAISY:	Scotland –
FIRST RED BIRD:	Is burning.
SECOND BLUE DAISY:	Scotland –
SECOND RED BIRD:	Is burning.
FIRST RED BIRD:	Pour –
ORANGE BIRD:	On –
FIRST BLUE DAISY:	Water!

FIRST RED BIRD:	Pour –
ORANGE BIRD:	On –
FIRST BLUE DAISY:	Water!
SECOND BLUE DAISY:	Scotland –
SECOND RED BIRD:	Is burning!
FIRST RED BIRD:	Pour –
ORANGE BIRD:	On –
FIRST BLUE DAISY:	Water!
GIRL: [Clapping her hands]	That riddle you all gave us was fun! Give us another!

[The parts of speech huddle a minute, then form a line in any order.]

THIRD BLUE DAISY:	Days –
FIRST RED BIRD:	Found –
RED ELF:	After –
FIRST YELLOW FAIRY:	Dry –
FOURTH BLUE DAISY:	Dove –
SECOND YELLOW FAIRY:	Forty –
FIRST DAISY:	Land –
ORANGE BIRD:	Fortunately –
LITTLE GREEN ELF: [Peeks out from behind Daisy]	Don't forget me! [Working himself up to it very dramatically, announces] The –
BOY AND GIRL:	[Look at each other in puzzlement]
GIRL:	[Pointing] It would help if we knew who the rest of them are.

BOY: [*Pointing to the Yellow Fairies*]
You, tell us your names!

FIRST YELLOW FAIRY: Blue! Red! Low! High!
Three! Four! Wet! Dry!

SECOND YELLOW FAIRY: Ugly! Pretty! Short! Long!
Happy! Sad! That's my song!

GIRL: They must be Adjectives.

BOY: That's why they were so busy painting the nouns.
[*Turns to Little Green Elf and says*]
How about you, little fellow? Who are you?

LITTLE GREEN ELF: I'm Article.

BOY: That's why you stick so close to Noun.

GARDENER: There's another little fellow you haven't even noticed.

GARDENER'S WIFE: Come up here, Preposition. Don't be afraid now. Tell the children who you are.

RED ELF: *To* the mountain –
In the ark –
Over water –
Through the dark.
You know all *about* me.
You can't say much *without* me.

GIRL: In the riddle, he must be 'After'.

GARDENER: Here's another fellow you haven't named.

BOY: You mean the tag-along.

ORANGE BIRD: Loudly! Softly! First! Last!
Bravely! Boldly! Quickly! Fast!

GIRL: Why he's Adverb. That's why he was tagging along with the Verbs.

BOY: Now give us your riddle again.

THIRD BLUE DAISY: Days –

66

FIRST RED BIRD:	Found –
RED ELF:	After –
FIRST YELLOW FAIRY:	Dry –
FOURTH BLUE DAISY:	Dove –
SECOND YELLOW FAIRY:	Forty –
FIRST BLUE DAISY:	Land –
ORANGE BIRD:	Fortunately –
LITTLE GREEN ELF:	The –
GIRL:	I know.

[*This time she arranges the group and directs the sentence in the proper order. Each word takes its proper place. Then she directs them to speak.*]

ORANGE BIRD:	Fortunately –
RED ELF:	After –
SECOND YELLOW FAIRY:	Forty –
THIRD BLUE DAISY:	Days –
LITTLE GREEN ELF:	The –
FOURTH BLUE DAISY:	Dove –
FIRST RED BIRD:	Found –
FIRST YELLOW FAIRY:	Dry –
FIRST BLUE DAISY:	Land.
BOY:	Without us, they're all just words.
GIRL:	We have to add the magic that gives them order and meaning.
BOY:	That must be what Grammar is – putting words together so they tell us all something. We've been using it most of our lives without even knowing it.

GIRL:	But who is the pale blue fellow hiding behind that Noun? We haven't heard from him at all.
BLUE ELF:	I! You! You! I! We! He! It! They! We! She! [*Pointing as he speaks to indicate the proper people, etc.*]
BOY:	Why, he's Pronoun! And there's someone else we have not heard from. And who are you? [*Pointing to Conjunction*]
BROWN ELF:	I am the joiner of words, with an 'and' and an 'or', and a 'but' and a 'for'.
GIRL:	She's Conjunction and important, too.
BOY:	Let's make up a sentence ourselves and tell everybody where to stand.
GIRL:	Let's try to get them all in.

BOY AND GIRL: [*Think and whisper a moment, and then arrange the parts of speech*]

PARTS OF SPEECH: [*Take positions as directed by Boy and Girl*]

RED ELF:	Throughout –
LITTLE GREEN ELF:	The –
FIRST YELLOW FAIRY:	Wide – [*Takes hold of Second Yellow Fairy's hand*]
BROWN ELF:	And –
SECOND YELLOW FAIRY:	Wonderful –

[*All players who have said their words now point to Yellow Fairy.*]

FIRST BLUE DAISY:	World –
SECOND BLUE DAISY:	Grammar –
RED BIRDS:	Is used –
ORANGE BIRD:	Daily. [*Points to Red Birds*]

BLUE ELF: [*Peeks out from behind Blue Daisy and says sulkily*]
You forgot me.

GARDENER'S WIFE: [*Puts arm around Pronoun*]
Poor little Pronoun! You left him out.

BOY: So we did. Let's see. I have it! Try again!
[*He rearranges, slightly, the Parts of Speech and directs the sentence again.*]

RED ELF: Throughout –

LITTLE GREEN ELF: The –

FIRST YELLOW FAIRY: Wide –

BROWN ELF: And –

SECOND YELLOW FAIRY: Wonderful –

FIRST BLUE DAISY: World –

BLUE ELF: We –

RED BIRDS: Use –

SECOND BLUE DAISY: Grammar –

ORANGE BIRD: Daily –

PUNCTUATION: Period! [*Loudly*]

GIRL: We've had a lot of fun in Grammar's Garden.
[*Turns to Gardener's Wife, Gardener and Boy, and takes two of them by the hand*]
Come!

[*All four walk over to stage right to join the Parts of Speech and Punctuation.*]

ALL IN CHORUS: North or South or West or East,
Every man – but not one beast –
Walks in Grammar's Garden.
Question there your friend or foe.
Tell him what he wants to know,

Or beg his pardon.
English, Spanish, German, Greek,
Each human being who would speak
Must do with words some playing.
When parts of speech are in their stations,
They bring about communication,
And that's what we've been saying.

CURTAIN

THE MAGIC PITCHER

by Barbara Betteridge
from the Greek Myths

CAST *(variable – 10 to 14 plus chorus)*

PHILEMON (*Fi-lé-man*), an old man
BAUCIS (*Bauw-kis*), his wife
TWO STRANGERS:
HERMES or MERCURY, the young one. He wears a round winged hat and winged sandals and carries a caduceus, a winged staff with serpents twined around it.
ZEUS, The older one. He has thick wavy hair and beard, but no scepter or other identification. He wears a long faded mantle draped to leave his right arm and shoulder bare.
NEIGHBORS, well dressed
CHORUS, who may speak singly or in unison

ACT I

[*Setting: A crude cottage on a hill. Philemon sits on a bench in front of the cottage. Baucis kneels beside him. The Chorus is grouped at one side of the stage.*]

CHORUS:

> Day-long across the blazing sky
> Phoebus Apollo rides on high,
> Holds the reins of his plunging steeds
> Lest they plunge mid-ocean, or river reeds,
> Keeping them firmly on their course,
> O'er mountain and valley and water source.
> Day draws to a close, and at last they run
> Below the horizon. Gone is the sun,
> But his parting rays still fling their glow
> Over the mountain peaks below.
> Over a valley in far-off Greece
> Spreadeth a mood of sun-down peace.
> Philemon sits at his cottage door,
> And Baucis, his wife, kneels him before.

[*Philemon pipes a shepherd tune on his recorder as Chorus goes out.*]

PHILEMON: My fingers lose their skills at last.
              Think, Baucis, twenty years have passed
              Since I a shepherd in the hills
              Once piped my merry tunes and trills.

BAUCIS: Oh, Philemon, from far away
              I often joyed to hear you play
              Sweet tunes that winged o'er vale and hill.
              But then, your music cheers me still.

PHILEMON: When Phoebus' chariot comes to rest
              At sundown in the flaming West,
              Then ever again my fingers long
              To celebrate the hour in song.

              [*Angry voices in the distance*]

BAUCIS: But hark! What noise disturbs the peace?
              Will such commotions never cease?

              [*Philemon strolls a few steps and reports.*]

PHILEMON: The village folk complete their day,
              As oft before, with rougher play,
              Two hapless fellows on the road
              They now beset with jeer and goad.

BAUCIS: Our neighbors all are richer than we,
              But most unlearned in courtesy.
              Throughout the Phrygian countryside
              Our village is known both far and wide
              For treating every stranger ill,
              Who, weary and hungry, climbs the hill.

PHILEMON: They drive these two like mangy curs,
              Throw sticks and stones, and even worse,
              Cheer on the children. For each hit
              Reward them. Oh, I'm sick of it!
              But, Wife, have we a bit of bread
              To share with them? We have a bed.

BAUCIS: Alas, if I had known that guests
              Were coming, I'd have saved the best!
              I was too *lavish* with our sup,
              And all but crusts were eaten up.

But there's a bit of honey still,
And milk once more the jug to fill.

[*Leaves to prepare it. The two strangers arrive still followed by shrieking children, angry villagers and barking dogs.*]

PHILEMON: Welcome, strangers, welcome here!
Pray, stop with us, and have some cheer.

YOUNGER STRANGER: We thank you, that you better greet us
Than your neighbors who did meet us.

FIRST NEIGHBOR: Have at the beggar with a stone!
Throw the old one then a bone!

PHILEMON: Ah, will you never mend your ways?
Belike as beggar will <u>you</u> end your days.
If once the gods note your behavior,
Then will your riches lose their flavor.

SECOND NEIGHBOR: Old fool, you'd better hold your tongue,
Lest with your neighbors you get in wrong.

THIRD NEIGHBOR: They've always lived from us apart,
As if they thought them all too smart.
Yet see – their house is but a shack,
And every comfort do they lack.

FOURTH NEIGHBOR: Their land is but a rocky plot,
And poorer every day their lot
Because they give to knaves like these
Their moldy crusts and sour cheese.

[*All laugh mockingly.*]

FIFTH NEIGHBOR: Let beggars feed the beggars then,
Or starve together. Come on, men!

SIXTH NEIGHBOR: We in our homes will snugly wait
And leave them to their wretched fate.

[*They leave laughing.*]
[*Baucis has been coming and going, setting the table.*]

PHILEMON: Good Baucis, bid our guests to stay.
Prepare some cheer for them, I pray.

BAUCIS: Most welcome are you, sirs, to this.
                           It isn't much, but what there is
                           We gladly share. A crust of bread,
                           Some milk and honey, and a bed.

                           [*Younger stranger indicates the older one should sit. Himself leaps
                           nimbly over a bench, leans his strange staff against the wall, then
                           sits.*]

YOUNGER STRANGER: Today we were arisen and gone
                           Long ere the glow of rosy dawn.
                           You need not ask us twice, my friend.
                           We're hungry at our journey's end.

                           [*The two bow their heads a moment, then eat.*]

PHILEMON: You must be weary, too, although
                           With both of you, it doesn't show.
                           You both look fresh. And you, my son –
                           I hardly was so nimble, young.

YOUNGER STRANGER: There's nothing like a staff as aid,
                           And mine is rather artful made.

PHILEMON: To me a staff with wings is new.
                           Pray what may we be calling you?

YOUNGER STRANGER: [*Laughs*]
                           Since I am nimble, as you see,
                           Suppose you call me 'Mercury'.

PHILEMON: 'Mercury' – that name sounds odd –
                           For he is Hermes, and a god.
                           And who may your companion be?
                           Is his name wrapped in mystery?

MERCURY: [*Solemn for once*]
                           That must you ask the thunder gruff,
                           No other voice were loud enough.
                           [*Drains his bowl of milk*]
                           I say, my friends, delicious food
                           Is this. The milk is extra good.
                           My bowl is empty. May I have some more?
                           [*He picks up the pitcher and tips it to pour.*]

BAUCIS: Alas, it's gone! We ate before,
                     And ate too greedily, I fear.

MERCURY: [*Pouring two bowls*]
                     Fear not, good Baucis. There's plenty here.

                     [*Baucis and Philemon exchange glances of amazement.*]

ELDER STRANGER: [*To Philemon*]
                     I would inquire – was there not
                     In ancient times, a lake on the spot
                     Where yonder village stands below?

PHILEMON: I've never heard that it was so.
                     I've lived a long life in these hills.
                     An ancient wood the valley fills,
                     Except where there are fields to plow
                     And meadows both for sheep and cow.
                     I never heard there was a lake.

MERCURY: If I may, some milk I'll take.
                     Give me the jug and let me pour.

BAUCIS: But really, sir, there can't be more.
                     Neither is there any bread.
                     Pray have a bunch of grapes instead.

MERCURY: Why, Mother Baucis, it's a feast!
                     There's still enough for two at least!
                     Both milk and your good bread as well.
                     [*Pours two bowls*]
                     Why on a shortage must you dwell?

                     [*Baucis and Philemon again exchange glances of amazement.*]

ZEUS: Indeed your food is fit for a god.
                     'Tis far o'er fertile lands I've trod,
                     Yet seldom sampled better fare.
                     Your honey tastes like nectar rare.

PHILEMON: My bees may wander at their will.
                     They're not confined to this poor hill
                     Where we must eke our livelihood.
                     They're free to fly where the flowers are good.

ZEUS: How is it with your neighbors then?
Do they fare well, these brutish men?

PHILEMON: Their land is rich, and they are too.
They've servants all their work to do.
They spend their time at idle games,
At calling travelers bad names,
At meat and drink. Their only chores
Are counting up their heaping stores.

BAUCIS: Alas, they lack all piety,
They neither worship deity,
Nor gratitude the gods they show
For all the bounty they bestow.
And *you've* seen how they treat the poor,
And scornful drive them from the door.
Each time it happens must I fear
That punishment for them is near.

MERCURY: Of milk again I stand in need,
Good Baucis, if I may – indeed,
There's naught that so refreshes thirst,
Of travelers' woes the very worst.

BAUCIS: Good sir, it truly grieves me sore,
But this time there's not one drop more.

MERCURY: [*Pouring milk once more*]
Indeed, good Baucis, you mistake.
There's plenty, if we *all* partake.

[*Once more Philemon and Baucis exchange looks of amazement.*]

ZEUS: [*Drinks another bowl, then speaks*]
We thank your hospitality.
Did you say beds for us there be?

BAUCIS: Our beds are in the other room.
I'll show you there, if you will come.

ZEUS: And you, good friends, where will you sleep,
If both your beds for us we keep?

PHILEMON: As we have often done before,
Here by the hearth, upon the floor.
It's hardness ne'er disturbs our rest.
Zeus grant you peaceful slumber, guest!

BOTH GUESTS: [*Smiling*]

   May Morpheus send you pleasant dreams!

[*All leave, Zeus in dignity, Mercury trippingly. His staff follows him of its own accord if this is possible to arrange. Only Philemon remains. Baucis returns.*]

BAUCIS:

   Our guests are passing strange, meseems.
   Think you there's magic in that staff?
   As much milk as they both could quaff
   Came from this little pitcher here,
   And the grapes untouched appear.

PHILEMON:

   [*Looks into the jug*]
   By Hermes! Still the jug is full,
   And the pitcher icy cool!
   Strange doings we have seen, I vow!
   Or do we dream already now?

BAUCIS:

   I wonder much about our guests.
   Noble they seem, though poorly dressed.

[*They lie down.*]

PHILEMON:

   The gods protect thee while thou'rt sleeping –

BAUCIS:

   – Be over thee, their vigil keeping.

CURTAIN

ACT II

[*Alternates may be substituted in the lead parts, if desired.*]
[*Thunder is heard in the distance. The curtain opens to reveal the Chorus in front of the cottage.*]

CHORUS:

   Great Zeus, "who rolls the hollow thunder,"
   In the night has wrought a wonder.
   Where a town at evening spread
   Lies a limpid lake instead.
   The village folk, far from their wishes,
   Flit therein as finny fishes.
   Zeus poured his anger on their town
   And his thunder struck them down.

[Exit Chorus]
[Philemon comes out of the cottage, stretching. Looks up.]

PHILEMON: The clouds are parting overhead.
             Ill weather today we need not dread.
             Phoebus Apollo lights the East
             With his flaming rays at last!
             [He pauses, sits down on bench and picks up his recorder.]
             Though stiff, my fingers ever long
             To celebrate this hour in song.

[Plays recorder. Baucis comes out. Looks at Philemon.]

BAUCIS: Some breakfast I must quick prepare,
             With our honored guests to share.
             By their magic bread was left,
             Or we should have been bereft.

[Zeus and Mercury appear in the background.]

ZEUS: Good morning friends. Pray, what's the weather?

MERCURY: Let us look outside together.

PHILEMON: Great Phoebus did in splendor rise,
             And now o'er hill and valley lies
             The radiance of his morning light.
             But – what has happened to my sight?
             The village should lie here before,
             But lo! A lake laps near our door!

[Baucis runs forward a little and looks below.]

BAUCIS: What do you say? A lake? Great Zeus!
             Was that the rolling thunder's use
             That in the night disturbed our sleep?
             Where are the neighbors? And their sheep?
             Their houses, cattle, servants all?

[Light thunder is heard again.]

ZEUS: I fear they're gone beyond recall.
             O'er gentle earth they *careless* trod,
             Nor turned their hearts toward any god.
             But now they know the Olympian's wrath!

78

Zeus found them out. 'Tis he who hath
Ordained their future life for them.
 – As fishes in the lake they swim –
The lake that long ago lay nigh
Once more reflects the purple sky.
But better *you* deserve, good friends.
For your hard lives, I'll make amends.
'Tis not for you to swim as fishes.
Instead, I'll grant your first two wishes.

[*Philemon and Baucis take hands. The curtain closes behind the four players.*]

BAUCIS:

If we could have somewhat to spare –
With travelers a bit to share –

PHILEMON:

We'd be most glad if neither need
The other one in death precede.
Together long our lives have twined.
Together may us Death, too, bind.

ZEUS:

It shall be so. – And now, turn 'round.

[*The curtain opens again, revealing a fine painted building.*]

BAUCIS AND PHILEMON: [*Together*]

What stands before us on this ground?

BAUCIS:

Our cottage is no longer here!

PHILEMON:

How could our cottage disappear?

BAUCIS:

Here stands a palace, gleaming white!

PHILEMON:

A marble temple! What a sight!

ZEUS:

Call it a palace or a temple –
For many guests it will be ample.
Here may the traveler end his quest
For food and shelter and sweet rest.
Here may he praise his gods as well.
And henceforth you two here may dwell
And measure hospitality
That fits your generosity.
And now farewell!

MERCURY: Farewell!

BAUCIS AND PHILEMON: Farewell!

[*Zeus and Mercury depart. Chorus enters.*]

CHORUS: So, gods did leave the ancient pair
                       A palace in their worthy care –
                       Atop the hill they'd loved so long,
                       Where Philemon had winged his song.
                       Here travelers from foreign lands
                       Received the best from Baucis' hands,
                       Who joyed she had so much to give
                       As long as there was left to live.
                       And then one morn when guests were there,
                       They missed the venerable pair.
                       In vain they hunted far and wide,
                       'Til suddenly two trees they spied
                       That stood beyond the palace door,
                       Where never trees had stood before.
                       "I am Baucis," the Linden spoke.
                       "I am Philemon," murmured the Oak.
                       "Baucis" – "Philemon" – "Baucis," they said,
                       Together the boughs that twined o'erhead.
                       And thus they were joined together in death,
                       As they had wished. For every breath
                       Of zephyr that sighed in the treetops tall
                       Made them thus to each other call.
                       Who knows if together still they stand
                       And welcome the stranger from foreign land?

                       CURTAIN

THE GOLDEN FLEECE

Presumed by Barbara Betteridge
from Greek Mythology

CAST

KING PELIAS
COURTIER
JASON
DAUGHTERS
YOUTHS
HERA
NINE ARGONAUTS
KING ÆETES
CHALCIOPE
MEDEA
TWO COLCHIANS
FOUR DRAGON'S TEETH
DRAGON
ORPHEUS
MINSTREL
CHORUS

[Enter Chorus]

CHORUS:

O hearken ye! Lo, here a tale is told
That stirs the blood and makes the heart beat fast:
A tale of noble deeds, of heroes bold,
And great adventure in a time long past
When Chiron, the old centaur, wise and mild
Reared among other youths King Æson's child,
Brave Jason, noblest of a noble band,
Who, when he heard his treacherous uncle's hand
Had seized the throne from Æson, rightful king,
Resolved to win it back nor let this thing
Remain unpunished. Now upon his way
Beside a stream, a woman old and gray
Bemoaned her fate. Brave Jason lent his might
And bore her over. Then before his sight,

Casting aside the cloak which her concealed,
Hera, the shining goddess, stood revealed.
"Hearken," she said, "and to my words give heed
I will befriend you in your hour of need."
She vanished. Then with courage kindled high,
Jason to the usurper's door draws nigh.

SCENE I

King Pelias' Court

COURTIER: Know you, O King, there stands a youth without
              Seeking admittance and beyond a doubt
              He means to enter. He is bold and strong.

KING PELIAS: Then bring him here. Perchance beneath some wrong
              He burns and wishes justice done. But go!
              Why tarry slave?

COURTIER: Alas, I do not know,
              But much I fear the sight of him will be
              Displeasing to you.

KING PELIAS: Fool! Bring him to me,
              If he mislikes me he'll be clapped in chains.

COURTIER: I go, O King! Zeus grant that for my pains
              No ill descend upon my luckless head.
              Ere this day's out I fear blood will be shed.

              [*Enter Jason*]

ALL: One sandal, see! His other foot is bare!

KING PELIAS: One sandal! Boy, who are you? Have a care!
              This is a sorry jest! You'd best beware.

JASON: Lo, I am Jason, Æson's son. This day
              I bid you by the gods your debt to pay.
              You turned my father from his rightful throne
              And left him wandering friendless and alone.
              All true men will I gather to my side
              And humble now your overweening pride.

KING PELIAS: [*Aside*] Young Jason, has he come to vex my peace?
                        I will dissemble, put him at his ease
                        And seek a way to slay him unaware.
                        [*To Jason*]
                        My dearest nephew! Full of joy am I
                        That you have sought me out. And my reply
                        To your demand, is that I've waited long
                        To give you back your kingdom. 'Twas no wrong
                        I did you, for I now return your land
                        Increased in wealth and peace into your hand.
                        Come sit beside me. We proclaim a feast.
                        All men shall come, the greatest and the least.
                        Come Jason! See, my daughters gather round
                        To do you honor, now that you are found.

DAUGHTERS: Welcome fair stranger, food and wine we bring
                        And in your honor shall our minstrels sing.

KING PELIAS: Are they not lovely? Choose one for your wife.
                        She shall be yours and tend you all your life.

JASON: I am o'erwhelmed: I little thought to find
                        Instead of enemies, true friends most kind.

KING PELIAS: Long have I waited this auspicious day.
                        Come minstrel, tune your lyre, strike up a lay.
                        Sing of the Golden Fleece, that noble prize
                        To which we ever turn our longing eyes.

MINSTREL: [*Sings*]
                        Long ago from out this land
                        Two children fair, in misery
                        Upon the back of a golden ram
                        Fled o'er the sea.

                        The girl was drowned in waters wild,
                        The boy in safety reached the shore
                        And in a grove he hung the fleece
                        Forevermore.

                        There, guarded by a dragon grim
                        That sleepeth not, it gleams afar.
                        What hero bold will win again
                        That golden star?

JASON: How beautiful and strange the minstrel's song;
                        It seems to tell of hidden hurt and wrong.

KING PELIAS: Ah, would that I were young and strong again,
                        I'd build a ship to sail the foaming main.
                        In Colchis would I win the fleece of gold!
                        But here there are no heroes as of old.

JASON: No heroes here? Then let *me* prove my worth.
                        I'll show you that of brave men there's no dearth.
                        Lo, I will sail to Colchis and will bring
                        The Golden Fleece back to this land, O King!

KING PELIAS: Well spoken, Jason! Noble youth go forth
                        Upon this quest and show all men your worth.
                        We'll help you all we can. Say what you need
                        And it shall be provided with all speed.

YOUTHS: Brave Jason, noble youth, now will we pray
                        The gods that they may send you on your way
                        With prosperous winds and grant you all success.
                        May Zeus himself this great adventure bless.

KING PELIAS: [*Aside*] Ha! To his death this hero I will send
                        And to that purpose all my aid I'll lend.
                        I shall be rid of him. No man alive
                        Who starts on such a quest can live and thrive.

CURTAIN

SCENE II

The Sacred Grove

[*Enter Jason*]

JASON: Here in this sacred grove the gods I'll pray
                        That they may bless and help me on my way.
                        This dreadful task I cannot undertake
                        Without their guidance. My chief prayer I'll make
                        To Hera, heavenly goddess. With her aid
                        I dare go forth and ever unafraid
                        Will find the Golden Fleece on Colchis shore
                        And seize it or return home nevermore.

[Prays]
O Hera, heaven's queen! Now hear my prayer
I seek thy help, I seek thy friendly care.
Without thine aid, I never can succeed
In this great task; and therefore to my need
Now lend thine ear. Tell me what I must do.
Guide thou my ship over the ocean blue.

HERA:

Jason, thou hero bold, now hark to me.
Within this grove there stands my Sacred Tree.
Take you a branch and place it on your ship,
For through it I shall speak; as from my lip
The words will fall to guide you on your quest.
Obey them as you would my own behest.
Go Jason forth, be steadfast, true and bold,
So shall in years to come the tale be told
Of how you sought and won the Fleece of Gold.

[Exit Hera]

JASON:

The gods are with me! Now the branch I'll take
From off the Sacred Oak, as Hera spake.
Through this the goddess will reveal her will;
Through this she shall our hearts with wisdom fill.

[Enter Argonauts]

ARGONAUT 1:

Jason, the ship is ready, all is done.
Her painted sides gleam brightly in the sun.

ARGONAUT 2:

The shore is piled with stores of every kind.
The shining sails prepare to meet the wind.

ARGONAUT 3:

The oars are ready, each man knows his place
And we like athletes longing for the race
Stand tiptoe waiting for our lord's command.

ARGONAUT 4:

One thing alone now daunts our eager band.
The ship's stuck fast and though we panting strove
Our work was all in vain, she would not move.

ARGONAUT 5:

What can we do? A ship upon the land
Is useless, though she ne'er so proudly stand.

JASON: Listen my friends, this leafy branch I broke
From off great Hera's tree, the Sacred Oak.
Hera herself appeared to me to say
This talking branch will guide us on our way.
Be silent all! Perchance the word divine
Will to each one of us his task assign
So that our noble ship may reach the tide
And proudly o'er the crested breakers ride.

VOICE OF HERA: The great ship stands
Upon the shore.
The restless breakers
Crash and roar.

Let Orpheus
Take now his lyre
And with his song
Your souls inspire.

Then will your ship
Majestically
Move down the strand
And ride the sea.

ARGONAUTS: Hera has spoken! To her words give heed.
The shining goddess is our help in need.

JASON: Come friends and heroes all, let us away.
Good Orpheus take thy lyre and raise thy lay
So that our ship, obedient to thy song,
May o'er the leaping waves bear us along.

[*Exeunt*]

CURTAIN

SCENE III

The Shores of Colchis

CHORUS: Long have the heroes ploughed the wine dark sea
Through many perils faced courageously.
Some of their number lost upon the way,
The Argonauts at last perceive the bay

Of Colchis' land. Now all their strength and wit
They need to find the fleece and capture it.
Lo, where the dark browed king advances slow
To meet the strangers and their will to know.

KING ÆETES: Who are you strangers, and what want you here?
               Come you in war? If so, 'twill cost you dear.
               My warriors with lawless men can deal
               And those who come to plunder and to steal.

JASON: O King, we do not come to rob your land.
               We are no pirates, but a noble band,
               The sons of heroes, sent upon a quest
               By Pelias, my uncle. As your guest
               I would appear, but though we come in peace
               We would bear home with us the Golden Fleece!

KING ÆETES: The Golden Fleece! Now tell me by what right
               You would bear off this prize? Without a fight
               We'll never let it go. But hearken ye,
               Let one among you all stand forth and he
               Shall speedily perform the tasks I name.
               If he succeed, he will win Fleece and fame.

               [Argonauts consult.]

JASON: Agreed, O King! Tell me what I must do
               We'll win through yet, although we are but few.

KING ÆETES: Come here tomorrow at the dawn of day
               And I will tell you what you must essay.
               Till then, return O warriors to your bark.
               Rest there in peace until the hours of dark,
               Fleeing before the coming of the light,
               Shall summon you to prove your worth and might.

               [King Æetes exits.]

ARGONAUT 6:   How can we hope these labors to fulfill?
               Without some aid it surely bodes us ill.

ARGONAUT 7:   And yet we cannot fight. Our band is small.

ARGONAUT 8:   Yea, in a battle we are bound to fall.

JASON: The tasks I'll try, and no more can I say.
                And if I die, perchance upon your way
                The King will send you and you'll see again
                Your homes and families across the main.

CHALCIOPE: How valiant are these men! How brave and strong.
                How can our father do so grave a wrong?
                Why should they die? If only they'd depart
                Far from our shores!

MEDEA: Nay, that's a coward's part
                And these are heroes from the lands of Greece.
                But I could help them win the Golden Fleece.
                If there is one among them knows no fear,
                Let him unto my counsel give good ear.
                Jason!

JASON: Who calls? Æetes' daughter here!
                Fair maidens, why have you remained behind?
                Your father hates us, are you of his mind?

CHALCIOPE: O no, we wish to save you. Go, I pray,
                And leave these shores ere dawns another day!

JASON: Nay, I have sworn your father's tasks to try
                And if I fail, why, then I can but die.

ARGONAUTS: And we'll die with you!

MEDEA: Listen while I tell
                What fearful deeds await you! You must quell
                Two fiery bulls who breathe devouring flame
                And yoke them to a plough and with the same
                Plough up this field and in the furrowed land
                Sow dragon's teeth from which an armed band
                Of warriors springs up. Then you must fight
                With everyone. This done you have the right
                To take the Fleece from off a mighty tree.
                'Tis guarded by a serpent, vast is he
                And ever watchful. So must you prepare
                To meet your death.

JASON: Nay, all this will I dare
                If you will help me with your magic art,
                The fame of which has spread to every part.

MEDEA:	Jason, I will! This box of ointment take.
	Anoint yourself as soon as you shall wake
	And nought can harm you, but you must have done
	Your every task before the set of sun.
	And one thing more. When from the broken earth
	The phantom warriors are brought to birth,
	Cast in the midst your helmet. Now away.
JASON:	Princess, my thanks. May all be as you say.

CURTAIN

SCENE IV

The Field of Ares

COLCHIAN 1:	See where the stranger ploughs the stubborn earth.
	His task is nearly done. He has no dearth
	Of courage. The fierce and brazen bulls are tame
	As yearling lambs.
COLCHIAN 2:	When hither first he came,
	Who would have thought his strength and power were such?
	Our King is frowning, this displeased him much.
KING ÆETES:	What magic has he found to give him aid?
	Sure to the gods much homage he hath paid
	Else had he been destroyed; no human might
	Could ere have done these fearful tasks aright.
ARGONAUTS:	The field is finished, half the work is done
	And still high in the heavens rides the sun!
ARGONAUT 9:	The dragon's teeth he's sowing now. Behold,
	He comes this way, brave Jason, hero bold!
	[*Enter Jason, sowing dragon's teeth*]
KING ÆETES:	Now we shall see, he cannot meet this band
	Of earthborn warriors. None can stay their hand.
MEDEA:	O may he but recall my words and throw
	His helmet 'mongst the phantom shapes and so
	Each will destroy the other. See they rise
	All armed, with hatred smoldering in their eyes.

[The warriors rise up. Jason flings his helmet among them.]

DRAGON TOOTH 1:   Who hit me? Clumsy lubber, was it you?

DRAGON TOOTH 2:   Nay, you hit me, I'll beat you black and blue.

DRAGON TOOTH 3:   'Twas I you struck! False traitor blow for blow
I will return.

DRAGON TOOTH 4:   'Tis only this I know:
No man shall strike me. There and there and there.

ARGONAUTS: Now all is finished! All the tasks are done.
By Jason's strength and prowess he has won!

KING ÆETES: What magic can have helped him? Ah, 'tis you,
False witch! This treacherous deed you'll rue.
Shame on your father's house you've brought. And I
Swear that if they shall win the Fleece, you'll die.

JASON: Now lead me to the Fleece ere in the west
The sun shall sink.

KING ÆETES: Nay, rather sleep and rest
You need before this last task you essay.
Let each man to his home now make his way.
We'll meet these heroes at the dawn of day.

[King Æetes exits.]

MEDEA: Bring your ship up river, moor her here.
At midnight's hour I will be standing near.
Let Jason and one other come with me
And I will lead you to the Sacred Tree.

ARGONAUT 1:   Let *me* go!

ARGONAUT 2:   No, let *me*!

ARGONAUT 3:   Let *me*, let *me*!

MEDEA: Orpheus must be the one. He is the King
Of Minstrels and can tame the savage thing
That guards the Fleece. Farewell, now must I go
And make all ready for the final blow.

CURTAIN

SCENE V

The Grove of the Golden Fleece

JASON:

There is the Fleece, quick let us seize it!

MEDEA:

No,
See where the dragon's coils about it go.
First must we silence him, then can you take
The golden prize, the treasure for whose sake
You have dared all. See where he turns his head.
Keep back until the monster I have fed.

DRAGON:

Who comes within my grove disturbing me?
I see some figures lurk mysteriously
Within the shade. I'll have them in my clutch
And crush their life out. Perish thus all such
As seek to steal away the Golden Fleece.

MEDEA:

O hush thee Dragon, hush thee, hold thy peace.
It is Medea; see what I have brought.
Food such as thou lovest and long hast sought.
Seek not to harm thy mistress, sink to sleep
And I will watch upon thy treasure keep.
[*Medea signs to Orpheus.*]

ORPHEUS:

Sleep, sleep! How blest
To take thy rest
From care set free
When shining star
Looks from afar
O'er land and sea.

Men close their eyes
With weary sighs
And sink to rest.
Their souls by thee
Are all set free
To sleep most blest.

MEDEA:

He is asleep! Quick, Jason, take the Fleece.
Away, away.

[*Jason takes the fleece and they hasten away.*]

CURTAIN

SCENE VI

By the Argo

ARGONAUTS: O hearken, here they come! Have you the Fleece?
       He has! O joy! Henceforth let sorrow cease.

ALL: [*In low voices*] Jason, brave hero, Jason noble Prince!

JASON: Hasten my friends, no time is to be lost.
       We must be off at once or it shall cost
       Us dear. One thing remains to do
       To thank the Princess. Fairest maid to you
       We owe our prize and nought we could achieve
       Without your help. So now we take our leave
       With hearts that overflow with thankfulness.
       But what is this? Now wherefore this distress?
       Your eyes are full of tears! What means it, say!

MEDEA: Ah, Jason, when you've gone upon your way
       I shall be killed. My father knows that I
       By magic art have helped you. So I sigh
       And tremble with an ever-growing fear,
       Knowing when you are gone my doom is near.

JASON: You need not die! Fly with us o'er the sea!
       Medea, come, and you my queen shall be.
       And you shall rule with me our favored land
       And all shall hearken to your least command.

ALL: Yea come, Medea, come! Without your aid
       The prize had ne'er been ours. Then come, fair maid:
       See where the Argo proudly lifts her head.
       Let us away! For lo! The east is red.

       [*Medea gives Jason her hand.*]

JASON: Here is the prize for which we crossed the foam,
       Won with Medea's help and now for home
       We're bound, and to the gods devoutly pray
       That they will help us on our perilous way.

       [*Hera appears.*]

HERA: Go, Jason and you Argonauts, go hence!
Your troubles are not ended; still immense
And fearful difficulties will you meet
Before your homes and wives again you greet.
Yet have you won your prize, the Fleece of Gold,
And none can wrest it now from out your hold.

CURTAIN

THE CASTLE OF THE KINGDOM OF THE STONES

by Barbara Betteridge
Amended and extended
From *The Blind Brethren* by Friedrich Hiebel

CAST

KING OF THE STONES
QUEEN, his wife
PRINCE, their son

ROCKS:
GRAVEL
MARBLE
LAVA
SANDSTONE
LIMESTONE
GRANITE

MINERALS:
QUARTZ
SALT
PYRITES
SULPHUR
MICA
FELDSPAR

SEVEN METALS:
QUICKSILVER
COPPER
IRON
TIN
LEAD
SILVER
GOLD

TWELVE PRECIOUS STONES:
OPAL
AMETHYST
TURQUOISE
AGATE
MALACHITE
GARNET
TOPAZ
ZIRKON
EMERALD
SAPPHIRE
RUBY
CORUNDUM

SPIRIT OF CARBON (later as
disenchanted DIAMOND)
FIRST GNOME
SECOND GNOME
HOST OF THE GNOMES

SCENE I

The Castle of the Kingdom of the Stones

[*Royal palace. King and Queen are seated on their thrones. In the background the scenery indicates mountain ranges, rock formations and caves filled with all kinds of crystals and precious stones.*]

KING:

The time has come. Our only son must go
To find the castle of the golden Sun.

QUEEN:

You're right, my husband. So he must. And yet
I fear some dreadful evil may befall him.
The way that he must go is long and lonely,
And the road beset with many dangers too.

KING:

No longer is our son a child, my Queen.
It is not right that we should baby him.
He is fourteen and he must learn to fight
And stand alone, to struggle with temptations
And win through strength his own, or fail and fall.
For first when he has proved himself a man
Will he be fit to be our kingdom's heir.

QUEEN:

Lo, here he comes. He seems to be prepared
To set about his journey. Yet he has no clue
What is in truth its purpose and its goal.

[*Prince enters.*]

PRINCE:

I come to bid you both farewell, my parents,
Before my journey leads me far away:
You, Father, who have filled me with your wisdom,
You, Mother, who have loved me tenderly.
Now I must serve the Earth, of all the Mother.
Now must I learn to read her book,
The marvel of her stones and crystals,
And wisdom of the stars that shine beyond her.
I'll not return until I find her light,
And find the castle of the golden Sun.

KING:

The way is long and lonely.

QUEEN:

And dangerous.

PRINCE:	I have no fear, dear parents. Eagerly Have I awaited this day of my departure.
KING:	Your eagerness is right. For you will need Much courage to triumph over all the dangers.
QUEEN:	And now before you go, one thing remains, My son – a secret we must share with you.
PRINCE:	A secret? Pray reveal it to me quickly!
KING:	It had to be concealed from you till now.
QUEEN:	It is the story of your birth, my son. You were not born alone, but as a twin. A sister shared the self-same stars with you. A lovely child she was, fair-haired – Oh, like a ray of light from heaven!
KING:	She disappeared, quite suddenly.
QUEEN:	And all these years, we've grieved for her in vain.
PRINCE:	A sister! How was she lost? Pray tell me all! Oh, do not hesitate!
QUEEN:	I hardly can continue –
KING:	Our lovely daughter was enchanted And by magic whisked away.
QUEEN:	It is a dreadful curse. But there is hope – One ray of hope. And this in you resides. For you alone can bring her back to us.
PRINCE:	There couldn't be a greater joy for me Than now to give my utmost to this task. Indeed, my heart is burning for the quest! Be sure I shall not come again without her!
KING:	Thy task is first to find the form Of her enchantment – her abode – And then redeem her.
PRINCE:	The task is a hard one.

QUEEN: Yet do not fear, my son. This ring I give you.
                         As long as you shall wear it, you will find
                         Protection from the evil spirits,
                         Who might enchant you too.

KING: Beware of them! For they are thick
                         Upon that pathway steep and treacherous
                         That leads unto the holy castle of the Sun.

QUEEN: Above all, never lose the ring!

PRINCE: A gleaming jewel on a golden ring!
                         It lends me wings of joy already.
                         In joy and freedom I depart!
                         Farewell – and wait in certainty, my parents –
                         My sister I shall bring!

[Exits with a parting wave]

CURTAIN

SCENE II

In the depths of the Earth

[*Cave of stalactites and stalagmites; in the background mighty rock crystals. Enter Host of Gnomes moving with staccato rhythm, tapping with their hammers and staffs, encircling the assembled rocks (which are stooping or kneeling figures entirely covered as yet)*]

PRINCE: [*Gives an offstage yodel-like call*]

GNOMES: Who knocks upon our portal?
                         Who has so hard a hand?
                         Seeks he our heavy hammers?
                         Or what is his demand?
                         All deaf we dwarves who live here
                         In gloomy depths of earth.
                         O rugged rocks around us,
                         O stones of greater worth,
                         Make answer to his call!

PRINCE: [*Coming nearer, slowly appearing. Addresses the assembled rocks*]
>Descending in the gloomy depths
>In blue-gray light, I only dimly see.
>Across my path stalagmites climb
>Like carven images. It almost seems,
>If I should touch one, it would come alive.
>Perhaps my sister is enchanted into such a form!
>Hallo!
>You jagged craggy rocks and angular!
>You cubes and hexagons!
>You pyramids triangular!
>Can no one answer here?
>Whose kingdom is it then,
>This gloomy cavern blue and cold?

>[*Prince raps on one of the silent veiled figures. It answers in a muffled voice.*]

GRAVEL:
>'Tis Mother Earth's,
>This kingdom built of rocks and ancient bones,
>Of crystals and of precious stones,
>And fragments of them all, like me.
> – But you disturb the busy gnomes!
>They've work to do. So quickly tell
>What brings you here, and then be gone!

PRINCE:
>To find the castle of the golden Sun –
>This is the purpose of my mind.

GRAVEL:
>This secret, only one who sees can tell.
>But I am Gravel. I am blind.
>Pray, ask another.

PRINCE: [*Raps on a white figure*]
>You, Marble – Even in a light so dim,
>Your beauty shines. You must know much of Earth,
>Perhaps of Sun as well.

MARBLE:
>Just as my mother, Limestone, does,
>I hold the secret hopes of ancient creatures
>Who left their shells behind to form my stone.
>These hope with me once more to see the Sun.
>We long for Man to come and lift us up
>To crown again some Sun-warmed hill,
>Like ancient Greeks, who raised a Parthenon

Of marble to crown their lovely city.
I look to *you* for hope. And *you* ask *me*?
My beauty I can lend you. Wisdom, never.

PRINCE: [*Rapping on a dark figure*]

Perhaps you, Lava, who surely boast no beauty,
Can offer wisdom in its stead.
Do you remember golden Sun?
And can you tell me where to find his castle?

LAVA:

Full well do I recall his burning heat,
When I as magma through the veins of Earth
In fiery liquid flowed.
But I am old and blind and frozen now.
I have nor eyes to see, like you,
Nor limbs to move and seek.

PRINCE: [*Rapping on a light-colored figure*]

And you, Sandstone, you lightest garment of the Earth —
Can you then tell me more than he?

SANDSTONE:

So long I've suffered
Throughout the history of darkened Earth,
I scarce recall my own beginning.
Sometimes the weaving welling waves
Have washed and worn my weary bones.
Sometimes a load of mountains bent my back.
Sometimes the everlasting scream and push
Of tireless winds have beat upon my body.
I'm old and weary, deaf and blind,
And neither wise nor beautiful.
I only ask: leave me alone!

PRINCE: [*Rapping on another light-colored figure*]

You, Limestone, mother of the Marble
And of many marvels more —
You who have decked this cave with gleaming beauty —
(For yours the jagged daggers of stalactites
That glance and glimmer overhead) —
In mountain ranges, valleys wide,
You look on many a sunny sky.
Do *you* know where to find the castle of the Sun?

LIMESTONE:

Eons ago, I felt the pull of Earth
And fell, an endless limestone rain;

Then lay through ages under dark sea-deeps
And softly gathered crispy shells –
Until gigantic hands and hammer blows
Upthrew me in tip-tilted heaps
On tumbled Earth, now long ago –
To build and mold a mountain here.
I never saw the Father Sun himself.
As by reflected light, the moon discloses
The secrets of the Sun, I see his image only.
But ask old Granite, the ancient wise one
Of the mountains. He knows all.

PRINCE: [*Rapping on a gray figure*]

You, Granite, eternal witness of the Earth's creation,
Tell me how to find the Sun and find my sister,
To disenchant this one who fell a victim
So long ago to evil spirits,
And ever since from us was hidden.
What do you know then?

GRANITE:

I am the strong hard table of the world.
My firm back holds the towering mountain ranges,
So Man can walk upon the Earth.
He builds me into mighty monuments
Defying wind and rain and sun and snow.
What did you say you wish to know?
I'm old and rather deaf.

PRINCE:

How old are you?

GRANITE:

I'm older than the other stones,
Older than Moon and Earth and planets, too.
But even I cannot recall the day
When golden Sun from darker Earth was riven
And did with shuddering pang depart for heaven.

PRINCE:

Oh, if you who are so old and wise
Can't tell me where to find the Sun
And where my poor enchanted sister,
How can I ever solve the riddle?

GRANITE:

Look at me, my wrinkled face,
The glitter of the mica in the midst,
Between the battle of the light of quartz
And feldspar's depth and darkness.

If you could read the answer there 'twere well.
If not, my silence must be answer.

PRINCE: Oh, riddles, only riddles, where'er I ask!
                 And here beneath the Earth 'tis only
                 Hammering of gnomes I hear –

GNOMES: Who knocks upon our portal?
                 Who has so hard a hand?
                 Seeks he our heavy hammers?
                 Or what is his demand?
                 All deaf we dwarves who live here
                 In gloomy depths of earth.
                 O rugged rocks around us,
                 O stones of greater worth,
                 Make answer to his call!

[*Enter Spirit of Carbon, black-veiled, with zigzag movement around the Prince*]

CARBON: You are still waiting for the answer, Prince?

PRINCE: I do, and eagerly I wait.

CARBON: You will wait in vain – those rocks are dull.

PRINCE: Dull?

CARBON: Yes, dull. Duller than you.

PRINCE: Dare you tease me?

CARBON: Dare not hope that you will ever find the way
                 – except through me.

PRINCE: What do you mean?

CARBON: With sureness I'll show you the
                 Way to the Sun.

PRINCE: Who are you – dark like ash and coal?
                 What can you do?

CARBON: More than you.

PRINCE: That is not much.

CARBON:	More than your parents.
PRINCE:	Not much that – either.
CARBON:	Mightier am I than all the Mountains. I'll show you the way!
PRINCE:	Guide me! Take me with you!
CARBON:	It is just nothing – hardly to be mentioned.
PRINCE:	What is it? Go ahead!
CARBON:	Ridiculous – just nothing, less than nothing – Give me your ring.
PRINCE:	That is impossible!
CARBON:	I must possess it.
PRINCE:	You ask in vain.
CARBON:	Why do you deny this tiny ring to me?
PRINCE:	Why do you ask for what I must keep?
CARBON:	No further question! It is you Who wants to know the way…
PRINCE:	My mother told me never to give the ring To anyone on earth.
CARBON:	Anyone – but me.
PRINCE:	You lie – you are an evil one. You cannot guide me further.
CARBON:	So perish then, and Devil's demons tend you! Dread beasts of prey attack and rip and rend you, Nor anguished prayer for mercy mend you! Hell will with hottest fire attend you, Its fanged snakes and stinging scorpions send you, Nor will anyone succor lend you! Again will icy fingers bind and bend you, Their chilling torments grind and spend you,

— Nor any being come defend you!
— If you go not with me —

PRINCE: [*Hesitant*]
I cannot give the ring.
— She did not mention you —

CARBON:
To me she certainly would give the stone.
I do not wish to keep it, only borrow.
I want to see its splendor all alone,
So trust me with it till tomorrow.

PRINCE: [*Reluctantly removes the ring*]
So be it then — but only as a loan.

CARBON: [*Jumping triumphantly, grabs the ring and puts it on*]
And now, lost child of Father Sun,
Your quest is over, though not won.
Ye gnomes come forth! Ye old deaf dwarves!
And cover him with Darkness' scarves!
[*Gnomes cover the Prince's head with scarves.*]
He broke the promise. Great the cost.
He will be blind — forever lost!

PRINCE: [*Beating the air in panic*]
What has befallen me? Where are
The crystal lights of Sun or star?
Within this gloomy cavern's blue
I see no faintest rainbow hue.
[*Stumbles, falls*]
Black is the world around me grown.
I bruise myself on every stone.
In vain with veils of gloom I wrestle!
Will I never see the Sun's great castle?

GNOMES: [*Encircling the Prince*]
That you could save us was our mind.
You're now, like us your brethren, blind.

CURTAIN

SCENE III

The Castle of the Kingdom of the Stones

[*Setting as in First Scene. King and Queen on their thrones. Assembled Minerals.*]

KING:
It's seven years ago now, our son left us,
To seek the castle of the golden Sun –
Nor any word we've heard in all this time.

QUEEN:
In seven years, he's failed to find his sister
And would not come without her.
Who knows if he still lives, or if some curse
O'ertook him too, and now as silent stone
He rests in earthy tomb unknown.

KING:
We've asked of Granite, Lava, Limestone too,
Of rocks and ridges, cliffs and caves.
I hardly know now, where to turn.

QUEEN:
Let's ask the Minerals what they know.
[*Calling to offstage*]
Ye Gnomes in caverns far below –
Lead up the Minerals! Let Quartz
And Salt and Pyrites here appear!

[*These enter, Pyrites dressed in dull gold and walking heavily, Salt in a white cubic box, Quartz in white robes and, if possible, his crystal form suggested, walking with dignity.*]

GNOMES:
We heard you calling, Queen and King,
And haste the Minerals to bring.

KING:
Let's ask Iron Pyrites if he knows
And will the Prince's whereabouts disclose.

PYRITES:
You ask of me, despite my name?
"Fool's Gold" I'm called, for 'tis my fame
To lure poor fools with golden glimmer –
Though Sulphur 'tis, not gold, that makes me shimmer.
But I've Iron too that gives me weight.
In Michael's sword it sealed the fate
Of that old dragon who played lord
In sulphurous deeps where once he roared.
But no one listens to my hints.

– Fools I've seen plenty, but no Prince.
Yet Sulphur summon, I suggest.
Of fiery depths of Earth 'tis he knows best.

QUEEN: Bubble, bubble, boil and smell!
                        Burning brimstone deep in hell –
                        You, yellow Sulphur, I summon here!
                        Condense to crystal and appear!

SULPHUR: [Appears in a flash, dressed in bright yellow, his gestures suggesting a demonic
                        quality, with a mocking bow]
                        You called, Your Royal Majesty?
                        What is it that you wish from me?

QUEEN: Pray tell us, have you seen our son?
                        Since seven years, he's lost and gone.

SULPHUR: And if I knew, you think I'd tell?
                        For all of me, he can burn in – well?
                        [Spinning around and laughing diabolically, disappears]

KING: [Turning to Salt]
                        You cube, the founding form of Earth,
                        Of modest mien and princely worth,
                        You who lend our food its flavor –
                        You Salt, I beg, grant us your favor.

SALT: [In a humble, friendly way]
                        Indeed, I should the matter know.
                        For no man in the world may go
                        Beyond my reach. Within Earth's crust at home,
                        Still through the seven seas I roam,
                        Where finny fishes flit or fly,
                        Where animals, where birds on high.
                        As in the seas, so in the blood of man:
                        To live without me, no one can.
                        I'll call your son. We'll find him soon, I trow.
                        [Calls offstage]
                        Hallo! You, Prince of Stones, make answer now!
                        [Silence]

KING: Alas, there's no one left but Quartz.

QUEEN: [To Quartz, who is standing off in a corner]
                        Approach, I beg you, honored stone,

First born of light, still ever bright,
The fate of our poor son make known.

QUARTZ:
Your son, alas, I haven't seen,
Despite my eye of crystal keen,
But you, look through my window clear,
And see if you can find him here.
[Quartz holds up his arm, a thin veil falling from it. Queen rushes to look through his "window." Quartz calls offstage.]
If anyone the Prince has seen,
Knows where he is, come tell the Queen!

[Spirit of Carbon suddenly appears in the background with zigzag movements.]

CARBON:
He – here – he there – he, he, and always he!
Is he not there – then he is here – in me!

PYRITES:
'Tis Carbon, from the darkest mine!

SALT:
For our late Prince a fateful sign!

PYRITES:
A dreadful doom will us consume!

KING: [Reflectively]

Though now his visage dark and drear,
Of yore he different did appear.
He used to deck the Earth with green,
In tallest trees reach toward the Sun,
And Sun's own light transform within
To living substances. Now under curse,
He dwells below, in darkest Earth.

QUARTZ:
Now sooty, he's banned to darkest mine.

QUEEN: [Who has looked aghast ever since Spirit of Carbon appeared]
– For my dear son, a dreadful sign!
This frightful creature – could he be
My son, condemned to misery?
Oh, curse of Carbon rock – I die!
[She faints. Salt and Pyrites rush to her aid and hold her.]

KING:
O steadfast Quartz, on you I must rely.
My castle falls. My Queen may die.
Bethink you, faithful servant, well.

Is there no one can break the spell
That binds my kingdom in its throes?
Who holds the answer? Pray, who knows?

QUARTZ: You've asked the rocks of many lands,
The girding mountains, flowing sands,
The Minerals, one after one.
Pray ask the Metals, ere you're done.
Each is companion of a wandering star,
Wiser than we are they, by far.

KING: Well spoken, faithful Quartz! Call them at once —
And seek the riddle of the woeful curse.
Ere it bring my realm to death — or worse.

CURTAIN

SCENE IV

Forest in the High Mountains

[*Mines of various metals, in the background, crystals and gems.*]

PRINCE: [*Blind, enchanted as coal, enters slowly and stumbles over a gnome*]
             I fall again — woe is me — oh, you have hurt me!

GNOME: Hie — watch your step.

PRINCE: Who are you who hinder me? I hurry —

GNOME: To Hades!

PRINCE: Heavens, where am I?

GNOME: Certainly not at home — secure on earth.

PRINCE: Who speaks?

GNOME: Who asks?

PRINCE: Who are you?

GNOME: Not yourself.
Collect your bones—and put them on a shelf.
[*Exits*]

PRINCE: [*Walks further, meets another Gnome, falls again*]
What language do you speak? Oh, impish trick!

SECOND GNOME: The Prince is lost – his mother deathly ill!

PRINCE: Dwarf, creature, flighty fellow, listen, stand!
Where is the way to my desired land?

SECOND GNOME: Closer than you might dream, deep in a mine.
The metals there will answer through their shine.

PRINCE: Tell me more, you grow now friendlier, gnome.

SECOND GNOME: You better watch your step and hurry home.

PRINCE: He also mocks at me –

SECOND GNOME: And mocks in vain.
[*Exit*]

[*Spirit of Carbon appears.*]

CARBON: Has no umbrella in the midst of rain!

PRINCE: Why do you follow me, so near, so far?

CARBON: Try – run away from me – to another star!

[*The seven Metals now appear and build a semicircle behind the Prince
and the Spirit of Carbon.*]

THE METALS: Be silent, goblins, gnomes, ye mocking dwarves!
The time has come for him to break the spell.

QUICKSILVER: I am Quicksilver, the air among metals.
I lend you my breath,
The speed of my running,
The gaiety.

PRINCE: Oh wonder, what a breath from stars in heaven!

CARBON: [*Like an evil echo*]
Breathe it – the air. I will poison all your lungs.

COPPER:	I am Copper, the warmth among the metals. I give you my red blood, The fire within your veins, The piety.
PRINCE:	I feel the warmth, it blesses me.
CARBON:	I change the blessings to a curse, oh coward.
IRON:	I am Iron, the strength among the metals. I give you my will power, The aim of your life, The constancy.
PRINCE:	This is the sword I need to kill out evil.
CARBON:	And turn the iron spear against yourself!
TIN:	I am Tin, the flash among the metals. I give you my feeling, The solemnity.
PRINCE:	Oh, I feel strength and courage growing more and more.
CARBON:	To kill you surely with your iron weapons.
LEAD:	I am Lead, the heaviness among the metals. I give you gravity Within your bones, The measure.
PRINCE:	I stand now on my own – in constancy.
CARBON:	I scarce can catch you – stand – remain, be silent!
SILVER:	I am Silver, the brain among the metals. I lend you force of thinking, Within your eye, The wisdom.
PRINCE:	I understand your word, your sacred tongue.
CARBON:	What do you say – repeat it – what – how – why?

GOLD: [*In the midst of the seven metals, which build the semicircle*]
I am Gold, the heart and the sun among metals.
I show you the way and the life
If you will go with me,
For I am the truth.

PRINCE: I will follow you. Oh rescue me, redeem me!

GOLD: Stretch out your hand and touch me.

PRINCE: [*Touches Gold*]

CARBON: [*Crying out*]   It hurts me – oh, I cannot stand it!
This radiance, this light – quick away – away –
That no one catch me and my ring.
[*Runs away*]

PRINCE: Redeem me from my curse.

GOLD: Bring back the ring you lost.

PRINCE: How can I bring it back? Oh, I am blinded.
My blinded eyes will never glimpse the demons
In vain – in vain.

GOLD: You must fight for me.

PRINCE: How can I?

GOLD: If you perceive that which I am.

PRINCE: Reveal your secret, Gold!

GOLD: [*Coming into the foreground of the stage*]
Become as strong as I, that no one break you.
Become as ductile as I am,
As malleable and insoluble.
Be genuine and true.
Stand upon your own,
Unchanging in mind and color,
Do not tarnish.

PRINCE: I promise you that I will strive to become as you.

GOLD: You speak a holy oath.
Know, now, your mother swoons and lies
In slumber, dangerously ill.
Hurry to bring the ring in safety back to her
Or she will die and all of you shall perish.

CURTAIN

SCENE V

The Castle of the golden Sun

[*The various forms of the Crystals in precious stones under the starry sky. The Prince, still covered by black veil, is led by Gold. At a distance Spirit of Carbon follows, bearing chains, and remains in background.*]

PRINCE: Where am I? Everything is strange about me.
I feel the empty ache of loneliness.
Has everyone forsaken me?
– Father, Mother, and Mother Earth herself
With all her rocks and minerals?
– You, Gold, alone still lead me on my way.

GOLD: Behold the realms of crystals and of gems.
The metals are your steps which lead to Heaven,
To your true home.

SILVER: [*From the left*]
The portal of the Moon.

QUICKSILVER: [*From the right*]
The staff of Mercury.
[*Gives him the staff*]

COPPER: [*From the left*]
The belt of Venus.
[*Gives him the belt*]

IRON: [*From the right*]
The sword of Mars.
[*Gives him the sword*]

TIN: [*From the left*]
The scepter of Jupiter.
[*Gives him the scepter*]

LEAD: [*From the right*]

        The shield of Saturn.
        [*Gives him the shield*]

GOLD: [*From the center*]

        The crown of the Sun.
        [*Puts the crown on his head and takes away the veil from the head of the Prince while the Precious Stones appear about him*]

(*A small class may have to borrow a group of precious stones from another class, or close the curtain long enough to assume quick costume changes, such as paper crowns, each with an appropriate gem painted on the front.*)

PRINCE:

        As precious stones I find in Heaven,
        Fresh powers all my limbs enliven.
        Once more my eyes are open wide
        And marvels see on every side.
        O'er me there steals a breath of grace.
        – What transformation's taking place?
        [*The Precious Stones appear one after the other as disenchanted dwarves.*]
        Garnet glows with ancient fires,
        While Ruby's radiant red inspires.
        Emerald gleams with wisdom's light,
        While Topaz beams with yellow bright.
        Turquoise mirrors blue of Heaven,
        While Agate smiles, with temper even.
        Zircon's gift's transparency,
        While Amethyst brings piety.
        Sapphire glows with faithful blue,
        While Malachite is green in hue.
        Opal's magic fire enthralls.
        Corundum's hardest of them all.

CHORUS OF TWELVE PRECIOUS STONES:

        Behold, we are the eyes of Earth,
        The glittering windows through which
        Spirits of the World look down.
        They watch and wonder at what is growing yonder.
        And we, the Twelve, watch *with* them.
        We wait for you, Thirteenth,
        Harder than we all, more splendid, too,
        Because you've formed yourself.

PRINCE: [*Kneels down.*]
You make me humble, Precious Stones.
No more than dust am I, no more than Carbon.
Yet as you bring me heavenly gifts,
The source of light within me grows,
And I am freed from Evil's bonds.

[*Spirit of Carbon rushes forward, dragging her chains.*]

CARBON:
He kneels in humble prayer.
Now is the time to kill him.
Snatch his sword, his crown and belt!

PRINCE:
Kneel down with me and worship our Redeemer!

CARBON:
Why should I do so, who am not redeemed?
Who is there to redeem me?

PRINCE:
You ask me for redemption,
You who seem to be my cursed shadow?
[*Stands up*]
I see you now! You are the sooty likeness of myself.
[*Embraces her*]
I love you!

GOLD:
You've read the secret of the Sun.
Your journey's over. Your quest is won.
It's time to free your sister here,
[*Points to Carbon, still dragging her chains*]
And bring your parents' hearts good cheer.
Conquer! Break the evil chain!
And as King begin to reign!

PRINCE: [*Taking Carbon's hands*]
O you, my twin, in darkness bound –
At last, my sister, you've found.
[*Takes out his sword and holds it up*]
Slumbering sun, though darkness hid you,
Through Iron's sword, of chains I rid you!
[*With his sword, slashes the chain, frees his sister*]
Blessed is this hour of disenchantment!

[*All the Precious Stones come and encircle the Prince and the Spirit of Carbon. While they speak in chorus, the garments of the Spirit of Carbon fall off and the brilliant form of the Diamond appears.*]

CHORUS OF PRECIOUS STONES:
> Oh, see the wonder! Carbon changes now,
> Transforms in crystal light. O all you stars,
> Rejoice in radiance, lend your colors!
> Lo, Diamond, the queen of all the gems –
> Behold her now, pure carbon, disenchanted!

PRINCESS: [*Disenchanted Spirit of Carbon now appears as Diamond*]
> Ah, Brother, long I awaited you in vain,
> Encased in darkness, bound in pain!
> Yet no one knows such happiness
> As one who's suffered long distress.
> Here is your ring, O faithful brother mine.

PRINCE: [*Giving her his crown*]
> And here your crown.

[*King and Queen appear on stage in happy reunion.*]

QUEEN:
> O children, you have now returned
> Unto the castle of the golden Sun!

KING:
> You rule now both together in
> Your Kingdom.

QUEEN:
> – A sacred sign and symbol
> For all of us until the end of time.

KING, QUEEN, PRINCE AND PRINCESS:
> Black Carbon can become a Diamond.
> So can the deepest darkness grow to light.
> So can the Earth, the dark and dusty one,
> So can our Mother Earth become a Sun!

ALL PRECIOUS STONES, METALS AND CRYSTALS:
> Clear as a crystal, transparent and bright,
> God's wisdom shines from eternal height.

CURTAIN

THE SACRED FLAME

Story taken from *Christ Legends* by Selma Lagerlof
Dramatized by Barbara Betteridge

CAST

FRANCESCA
JACOPO DEGLI UBERTI, her father, a weaver
TADDEO, her brother
RANIERO DI RANIERO, who marries Francesca

FRIENDS OF FRANCESCA:

      GINEVRA
      LUCIA
      GABRIELLA
      TERESA
      RENATA

WEAVERS:

      PIERO
      GIUSEPPE
      ALFREDO
      RICARDO

THREE SQUIRES:

      GIOVANNI
      GIACOMO
      BENVENUTO

FOUR KNIGHTS
A FOOL
FOUR ROBBERS
TWO PILGRIMS
A WIDOW
THREE PEASANTS
ODDO
A BISHOP
A PRIEST
A MOB: PILGRIMS, TROOPS, MERCHANTS

ACT I

SCENE 1
A room in Florence near the end of the Eleventh Century

[*The simple furnishings must include a bird cage occupied by a reasonable facsimile of a quail. Five girls, Ginevra, Lucia, Gabriella, Teresa and Renata are visiting Francesca who is seated, sewing on a large piece of cloth-of-gold.*]

LUCIA: What are you sewing, Francesca, pray tell, that you are stitching it so carefully?

FRANCESCA: It's from a bolt of cloth-of-gold my father got from Venice for the countess. She didn't need it all. I begged for this.

LUCIA: It looks in truth like the captured glow of the sun itself, when you hold it so.

TERESA: Our poetess, Lucia! [*Others laugh*] It's big enough to make a tent!

RENATA: [*Poking her finger playfully into the bird cage*]
                    Or cover a royal elephant!

FRANCESCA: It's meant to be part of my wedding dower.

GINEVRA: Oh, tell us the day!

GABRIELLA: Tell us the hour!

FRANCESCA: The wedding day is hardly set.

TERESA: She hasn't told us the man as yet.

RENATA: To guess, one needn't be so wise. Haven't you seen her making eyes at bold Raniero?

GINEVRA: That's hardly fair! I'd say it's Raniero who seems to wear his heart on his sleeve for all to see.

GABRIELLA: Raniero! My dear, how lucky you are! He's the bravest man in Florence!

TERESA: Brave if you like a braggart. I don't!

RENATA: He hasn't asked your hand, my dear.

118

GABRIELLA:	Remember the time Fogotto stored a load of grain upstairs in his house, and a loft beam bent? If Raniero hadn't been there and lent his strong back and arms to hold up the frame, the roof would have fallen.
GINEVRA:	The carpenters came with another beam to hammer and hack, while Raniero held up the house on his back!
RENATA:	They say he took on twelve rogues in a fight in the street one day and they all ran away!
TERESA:	Who wants to marry a fellow who fights at the drop of a pin, for imagined slights?
GABRIELLA:	Raniero's the handsomest man in Florence!
RENATA:	Oh no! He has such a scar that disfigures his face!
FRANCESCA:	I find him strong and kind and good, although he's not always understood.
RENATA:	Wasn't there another fellow who had a mind to marry you?
TERESA:	The cripple in Raniero's shop, who walks with a lunge and plunge and stop.
GABRIELLA:	Lorenzo, Oddo's son. Upon my life, he'll never get a girl to wife!
FRANCESCA:	He is gentle, kind and true. I wouldn't hesitate to marry him, except I love Raniero.
GINEVRA:	What are your wedding plans, my dear?
GABRIELLA:	Yes, tell us, Francesca – we long to hear!
FRANCESCA:	Raniero will speak to my father tonight.
LUCIA:	I fear the idea will hardly delight your father. Raniero's reckless and wild.
FRANCESCA:	[*Sighs and holds up the cloth-of-gold*] My love is so shining, it will never dim, and I'll never marry any but him.

CURTAIN

SCENE 2

A room similar to the setting for Scene 1, but rearranged

[*There is a damaged picture on the wall; there is no bird cage. Francesca is sewing again on the cloth-of-gold. Ginevra enters.*]

GINEVRA: What! Francesca, sewing still?

FRANCESCA: [*Jumping up, dropping the cloth and taking Ginevra's hands*]
Welcome, Ginevra! [*Sighing.*] I'll never finish this! Our wedding came so suddenly, and since, I haven't found the time.

GINEVRA: I think you love this cloth-of-gold.

FRANCESCA: Yes, it shines so like my love – each hour seems brighter from its glow.

GINEVRA: Forgive my saying it – Raniero's not an easy man to live with, I should think. [*Glances up and notices the mutilated picture*]
What's this?! Your painting of the Caratas hangs full of holes and tatters!

FRANCESCA: Yes, I meant to take it down. I'll do it now. Raniero's gone.
[*Removes the picture from the wall*]

GINEVRA: [*Suspiciously*] It looks as if a hunter armed with bow and arrows had made it his unworthy mark.

FRANCESCA: It's hard, you know, when you are strong and brave and young and have to ply a boring trade all week – then Sunday is a rainy day. Like a lion in a cage, he paces back and forth, until he finds some pastime to engage him. It's good the rain has stopped, and he could go outside again. This picture was a gift, elsewise I wouldn't hold it any treasure.

GINEVRA: He comes! Raniero's step I recognize. My sweet, I'll quickly say addio! [*Kisses Francesca and leaves as Raniero enters*]

RANIERO: My aim's so good, I'll never fail! Guess what Francesca! I even shot your quail. I took a stand and bade the page to free her of her golden cage. I brought her down – like that! [*Snaps his fingers*]

FRANCESCA: My quail Bibatta, you have killed to prove your aim? Raniero, she so soft and sweet, who from my hand was wont to eat!

RANIERO:　　　　　There's no way in this wretched city for a man to gain renown.
　　　　　　　　　　Making armor is a stupid trade – I'd rather wear it once it's
　　　　　　　　　　made. – If I could find a king to serve! [*Exit*]

FRANCESCA:　　　　My love for him I must renew and not bedew this golden cloth
　　　　　　　　　　with useless tears. – Good Jesu! Is that a hole I see, or a shadow,
　　　　　　　　　　fooling me?

CURTAIN

SCENE 3
A small room

[*There is a counter covered with bolts of cloth and great spools of yarn. There is a door in the background through which is heard the clatter of looms from a room beyond. Francesca's father, Jacopo degli Uberti, is seated at the end of the counter, his head in his hands. His friend Piero enters.*]

PIERO:　　　　　　My friend, you seem distressed. What's troubling you? [*Jacopo remains silent. Shakes his head sadly*] Nay, I can guess. Raniero's rumors flitter-flutter from the tavern to the gutter.

JACOPO:　　　　　My fellow weavers turn their faces from me on the street.
　　　　　　　　　　Disgraces on our family he heaps each day. Francesca hardly
　　　　　　　　　　sleeps.

　　　　　　　　　　[*Three weavers burst in, obviously angry. One carries a bolt of cloth.*]

GIUSEPPE:　　　　This cloth just came by messenger from Rome!

ALFREDO:　　　　　Rejected!

RICARDO: [*To Jacopo*] Feel it, Sir! It came from your shop, did it not?

JACOPO: [*Examining the cloth. Nods sadly*] Here is my mark.

GIUSEPPE:　　　　It is the second lot returned!

JACOPO:　　　　　I swear it is not my fault!

ALFREDO:　　　　　He sees there's hemp mixed in this bolt.

RICARDO:　　　　　I thought Raniero twisted facts in saying you mixed hemp with
　　　　　　　　　　flax. But here's the proof.

JACOPO:	A bitter pill it is, that friends believe this ill.
PIERO:	Let him offer explanation. We know Jacopo's reputation. It is as fair as anyone's.
GIUSEPPE:	It is a serious offense, Jacopo – this adulteration!
RICARDO:	You know that Florence is famed far and wide for textiles . 'Tis our pride, none others weave as well as we.
ALFREDO:	That one of us has secretly mixed hemp in with his flax reflects upon us all. We must inspect the goods and yarn you have on hand. Do you agree to this demand?
JACOPO:	My workshop boasts, like yours, two rooms. You know where you will find my looms. [*Giuseppe and Alfredo go into the adjacent room. Ricardo begins to examine the bolts and spools visible to the audience.*]
RICARDO:	Ah, here is one, and clear the fault! [*Alfredo and Giuseppe return in excitement.*]
GIUSEPPE:	We found one too! Now every bolt of cloth and every spool of yarn we've seen. Our duty 'tis to warn our customers what we have found.
ALFREDO:	Two bolts of cloth, and both unsound!
JACOPO:	At first you all befriended me, and all but one defended me when my linens came in doubt because of rumors spread about. Now I look for friends in vain.
RICARDO:	I always say that where there's smoke there's fire. It's not a fitting joke to take risks with our quality.
JACOPO:	I'm innocent! Just hear my plea! I've lived in Florence all my life. Here was I born, here took a wife. My family for a hundred years has dwelt here and been honored here.
PIERO:	No family is honored more. Why, 'twas his grandfather who bore the shield aloft that now adorns our church. No one can scorn such strength. The shield still hangs on high, reminding every passer-by of one of Florence's great men.

JACOPO:	It must have been a journeyman who works for me. I think of one who came from Pisa recently. His work's unsatisfactory. Some private gain he must have sought by putting hemp in where he ought to use pure flax. But otherwise I must believe when each denies his guilt who works for me.
ALFREDO:	The master is at fault, I say. The faster he talks. the more each rambling word betrays him. What think you?
GIUSEPPE:	We have seen the shoddy goods come through his shop. I say we must stop Jacopo before our reputations suffer.
RICARDO:	The weavers' guild must meet tonight, decide how best to put this right.
ALL:	We'll have no more to do with him. [*Exeunt all but Piero.*]
JACOPO:	A ruined man I stand, without a single friend.
PIERO:	Yes, one Jacopo. At your side, believing in you, I abide. This is Raniero's work. He first did sow the seeds of doubt. Some people like to stir up trouble, then stand aside and watch it bubble.

CURTAIN

SCENE 4
Same setting as Scene 3

[*Jacopo, sitting at his accounts, shakes his head sadly. Speaks to Taddeo*]

JACOPO:	Always the orders go to others now. They give me only what they easily can spare, and that is charity. – But surely it fares Francesca worse. How can she this man endure who's brought her family ridicule, her father grief. [*Pause*]
TADDEO:	Last week's adventure most stuck in my throat – I guess I've always felt a bit of swagger to think a forefather of mine had hefted that great shield so high on the cathedral wall – and now that insolent pup removes it. How am I to face my comrades now?
JACOPO:	If he would use his strength a wiser way, then Francesca might in turn be proud of him!

FRANCESCA: *[Bursts through the door, sets a bag on the floor and flings herself into her father's arms]*
O father, will you take me back? – Though little I deserve it, who have made you suffer so. – And Taddeo too!
[Taddeo runs out in questioning alarm.]

JACOPO: My roof is always yours – and both our hearts. But tell what new disaster is befallen that you have run through the dark streets alone, heedless of danger?

FRANCESCA: You haven't heard?

[Taddeo returns.]

TADDEO: Paolo was running up the hill. He told me all. When Oddo returned from work, he missed Lorenzo, and when he heard his dog barking wildly, in back of the shed, he ran there to find –
[He looks at Francesca hesitantly.]

FRANCESCA: Lorenzo dead!

TADDEO: He hanged himself.

FRANCESCA: Because of me!

TADDEO: Because of Raniero. Paolo said Raniero had ridiculed his limp this afternoon, had laughed at him for still hopelessly loving his wife, and had pushed him so he fell, hurting his crippled back.

JACOPO: *[To Taddeo]* Bar the door, Taddeo! He will surely come after her!
[Soothing Francesca] My poor little girl! We will protect you, with God's help. *[He adds this anxiously.]*

FRANCESCA: He will not come. It would not suit his pride. I know him – now. He will expect me to return – on hands and knees were best – and beg him for his favor. I shall not go.

TADDEO: I wish I were his match! I'd beat the good-for-nothing wretch!

FRANCESCA: *[Leaps toward him and puts her hand over his mouth]*
Don't say it! It isn't true! *[Her father and brother look at her dumbfounded.]*
No one will ever understand. I still love him! I still have faith in him – a little. I had to leave him ere I lost the last small glimmer!

CURTAIN

A street scene

[*A backdrop of painted houses, at least one of which has a balcony. Lucia and Ginevra enter stage right, while Renate, Gabriella and Teresa enter stage left.*]

LUCIA:	You haven't been to church yet?
RENATA:	We're just going.
GINEVRA:	We went early to light a candle and say a prayer for Uncle Giovanni. – He's very ill, you know.
LUCIA:	I confess I almost forgot poor Uncle, I was so distracted by what lay before the Blessed Virgin's image.
THE OTHERS:	Tell us, Lucia!
LUCIA:	You've never seen the like! You'll have to make up some excuse to kneel there, too, and take a look at it.
OTHERS	What? What?
GABRIELLA:	Another prize from brave Raniero?
LUCIA:	Indeed – a topaz brooch – a jewel that gleams [*pauses and sighs*] with all the high bright light of Heaven – in a simple setting made of hammered gold.
GINEVRA:	It must be worth a fortune!
GABRIELLA:	It couldn't equal the string of pearls he sent before!
TERESA:	They say that even Countess Matilda admired them.
RENATA:	Coveted them, would be a better word. They say her eyes turned green with envy and she near forgot her prayers to gaze on them.
TERESA:	No more than you did! [*Laughter*]
LUCIA:	I wonder where Raniero is?
GABRIELLA:	They say he is in the service of the emperor.
GINEVRA:	Commands a hundred men!

TERESA:	I wish I did. [*Laughter*]
LUCIA:	They wage campaigns in many foreign lands.
GABRIELLA:	He is so brave and bold, the finest prizes fall to him.
TERESA:	Some with blue eyes, I doubt not. [*Laughter*]
RENATA:	And auburn curls! [*More laughter*]
GINEVRA:	For shame, girls! I'm sure his heart is faithful to Francesca – in his peculiar way.
GABRIELLA:	Sweet Ginevra! You think the best of everyone.
GINEVRA:	He proves it by the prizes he sends to the Madonna. In his mind's eye, you may be sure, he sees the pearls around Francesca's neck, the brooch against her olive skin. He knows she'll see them, hopes she'll read their message and forgive him his former wildness.
OTHERS:	You dream!
RENATA:	It's clear you haven't heard the latest, all of you! Last month my husband's brother, Berto, came home wounded from crusading to save the Holy Sepulcher – he was with Godfrey of Bouillon. He says Raniero left the emperor and joined them in Constantinople, months ago now. His reputation as a fighter is second to none among them, as it was in Florence.
OTHERS:	Tell us more!
RENATA:	I don't know much, only –
OTHERS:	What? Tell us!
RENATA:	I'm not supposed to.
OTHERS:	Please! We promise not to tell!
RENATA:	It was Berto who brought the brooch for Raniero to the Duomo.

CURTAIN

ACT II

SCENE 1
A military camp

[*In the center is an improvised table consisting of a door on boxes. Raniero sits at one end facing stage left. Four other knights are seated around the table drinking. Before Raniero is a burning candle with some stones around it to make it stand. The main light in the tent is the flickering of torches, which probably can be arranged electrically. There is a sizable pile of treasures heaped at one side of the tent. Three squires are waiting on the knights.*]

1ST KNIGHT: What a triumph! [*The knights click their goblets together*] The Saracens are dead who kept us from the Holy Sepulcher!

2ND KNIGHT: Our arms have won the victory!

3RD KNIGHT: The Holy City's gutters run with blood!

4TH KNIGHT: [*Points to the heap of trophies*]
                 The infidels' possessions all
                 are ours, to do with what we will. Come, roll the dice again!

3RD KNIGHT: My win! [*Goes to heap of treasures and selects something*] This Persian rug shall decorate Cornelia's house and mine.

1ST KNIGHT: Just how do you propose to drag it home?

2ND KNIGHT: Perhaps he thinks that *it* will carry *him*! [*All laugh.*]

3RD KNIGHT: I'll go in state aboard a ship and pay my way with loot, as doth befit a hero.

2ND KNIGHT: There won't be ships enough to go around. We'll crawl home, inch by dusty inch, as we have come.

1ST KNIGHT: But wear our scarlet crosses on our backs as sign that we have won. How every town will fete us on the way, when we return as heroes!

   [*Raniero, who throughout the scene has been making occasional unexplained gestures, as though catching moths, now speaks to an elderly squire.*]

RANIERO: Benvenuto, fill our cups! I toast the greatest hero of the day, Sir Godfrey of Bouillon!

   [*Benvenuto pours drinks and the knights drink a toast.*]

3RD KNIGHT:	Tomorrow we will crown him!
RANIERO: [*Soberly*]	Nay, I've heard him say, when contemplating victory, he'd never wear a crown of gold where his beloved Lord wore one of thorns.
4TH KNIGHT:	Raniero, then! Let's crown him king!
3RD KNIGHT:	A doughty fighter!
4TH KNIGHT:	First over the wall he was, at Godfrey's side. He cut a swath of infidels falling like stalks of wheat!
1ST KNIGHT:	Yes! Have you seen? Godfrey so esteems him, he invited him to be the first to light his candle from the sacred ones that burn before the tomb of Christ!
2ND KNIGHT: [*Pawing through the loot*]	A crown! A crown for Raniero! What! Have we no crown in all this gold?
	[*A sudden gust from the tent's opening behind Raniero makes him shelter his candle for a moment, then turn. Enter Fool*]
RANIERO:	Who comes? – Aha, a fool! I've heard he is an entertaining fellow. Come, Sirrah, perform your tricks for *us*!
FOOL:	I know a story, but you wouldn't like it.
RANIERO:	Are you not small enough without belittling yourself? [*The others laugh.*] Go on, Fool!
FOOL:	You wouldn't hear me out.
RANIERO:	Indeed we will! I guarantee it! I'll cleave that fellow through [*makes a stabbing gesture*] who dares to interrupt! Proceed!
FOOL:	Once upon a day, our Lord and Saint Peter sat on the highest tower in Paradise and looked down at the earth. Our Lord kept perfectly still, but Saint Peter now clapped his hands for joy and now turned his head away in disgust, now laughed and now wept.

Our Lord asked, "What troubles you, Peter? Are you not pleased that Jerusalem has been rescued from the unbelievers?" |

"It is true that I have long looked forward to this day," Peter answered. "Yet now, I think it might better have remained as it was." [*Fool casts a furtive glance at the knights who begin to frown.*]

"Whatever can you mean?" asked the Lord. "Have not my knights risked their lives with utmost fearlessness and won the victory?"

KNIGHTS: Bravo!

FOOL: Don't interrupt me! Now I forgot where I left off. — Oh, yes!

Saint Peter asked, leaning out and pointing downward, "Do you not see those mounds of corpses, those smoking ruins? Do you not hear the wretched prisoners moaning in the night? Your brave knights are beasts and murderers! You had better have left the deed undone!"

[*The knights laugh raucously.*]

1ST KNIGHT: What, Fool! Is Saint Peter wroth with us?

RANIERO: [*Impatiently*] Come, come, Fool!

2ND KNIGHT: Be silent, let us hear if our Lord spoke in our defense.

FOOL: No, our Lord was silent. He knew of old that when Saint Peter had once got agoing, it wasn't worthwhile to argue with him. Saint Peter admitted that finally the knights had remembered to which city they had come and had gone to church barefooted and in penitents' garb. But he pointed out that that spirit had not lasted long.

Thereupon he leaned once more over the tower and pointed downward toward Jerusalem. He pointed out the Christians' camp outside the city.

"Do you see how your knights celebrate their victories?" he asked.

And our Lord saw that there was revelry everywhere in the camp. At first our Lord frowned. But then, looking directly toward one particular tent, he began to smile.

Saint Peter followed his gaze. Outside he saw two Saracens' heads mounted on lances – inside knights and squires drinking and roistering, as everywhere else.

"What pleases you so much in this tent?" asked Saint Peter, for our Lord's eyes were fairly sparkling with delight.

Saint Peter looked more closely at the hard faces of the knights. The host, a man of about thirty-five who sat at the head of the table, bore the most dreadful aspect of all. His frowning face was deeply scarred and scratched, and he had a loud bellowing voice to match it.

RANIERO: [*Trying to erase his frown*] You're a daring fellow!

1ST KNIGHT: Let us see what he is driving at.

FOOL: Now don't interrupt me! A fool forgets so easily what he would say. – Oh, yes. – Suddenly our Lord spoke. He asked Saint Peter if he saw wrongly, or if it could actually be true that one of the knights had a burning candle in front of him.

[*Raniero gives a start, glares and puts his hand on his sword.*]

Saint Peter could not help but pity the Lord. "You are mistaken," he said, "if you imagine this knight is thinking of Your sufferings and death. The candle reminds him instead of his own glory in the day's battle."

But our Lord contradicted Saint Peter quietly. "It is you who are mistaken. It is not an ordinary candle to him. – Don't you see how careful he is to guard that particular flame which he lit at My tomb?"

2ND KNIGHT: [*To the others*] The fool is right! Raniero's been more occupied chasing moths away from that precious flame than with his drinking! [*All laugh. Raniero grows angrier.*]

FOOL: Still, Saint Peter was doubtful. "You can hardly know this knight, My Lord," he persisted. "For he is not one to attend Mass regularly or wear out the prie-dieu."

"Saint Peter, Saint Peter," our Lord said earnestly, "I promise you, this knight shall become more pious than Godfrey. You will see Raniero di Raniero gently helping widows and caring for the sick and despairing, as he now cares for the Sacred Candle's flame."

[*All the knights laugh inordinately.*]

[*Raniero springs to his feet as though to reprove the Fool. In so doing he bumps the table and the candle topples. Controlling his anger, he takes time to set up the candle, then turns to rush on the Fool. But the Fool has escaped out the tent opening.*]

RANIERO: I'll settle my score with him another day.

3RD KNIGHT: [*Mockingly*] One thing is certain, Raniero. This time you cannot send to the Madonna in Florence the most precious thing you have won in battle.

RANIERO: And, pray, why not?

1ST KNIGHT: For the very good reason that your most precious prize is a candle flame.

2ND KNIGHT: You can't send that to Florence! [*Others laugh.*]

RANIERO: Zounds! That's just what I will do! [*He turns to a squire.*] Giovanni, make ready for a journey! Tomorrow you shall take this candle flame to the Duomo in Florence!

GIOVANNI: Not I, Sir. No fool am I. – And fool it would require. – Why, the flame would flicker out and die with the first gust outside the tent!

RANIERO: Giacomo, you will go! A pair of brown eyes waits for you in Florence – unless they've turned toward present company. [*Laughter*]

GIACOMO: Not I, Sir. My knee is game, unfit for riding any beast until it mends.

RANIERO: Ben! – Benvenuto!

BENVENUTO: H-here, Sir!

RANIERO: Are you deaf!

BENVENUTO: A l-little, Sir.

RANIERO: Since when?

BENVENUTO: I was this morning cl-clobbered on the ear.

RANIERO:	No doubt d-deserved it too! [*Laughter*] Pack up! You leave for Florence in the morning!
BENVENUTO:	N-not I, Sir! I'm not so brave and bold as you!
2ND KNIGHT:	You will have to go yourself, Raniero!
RANIERO:	Zounds, I will!

CURTAIN

SCENE 2
On the road from Jerusalem to Florence

[*For this and the following scenes, there is a backdrop on which a map is painted showing the route from Jerusalem to Florence. At the beginning of each scene a squire comes on stage with a pointer and indicates the spot on the map where the scene takes place. As this scene opens, Raniero is leaning against a pile of rocks, beside him, the burning candle. He draws a chunk of bread from a pouch and breaks it. Gazes offstage*]

RANIERO: [*Admiringly*] Those Saracens know their horses. Graze your fill, my fine Arabian. You won't always find even scanty grasses by the wayside. How reproachfully you look at me! Do you wonder at your master's snail-like pace, his mad way of riding backwards to shield a candle from the wind? Are you trying to tell me you were born for greater adventures? A swaybacked mare could carry such a candle! And a woman could have made the easy ride past Joppa. But wait! It will yet be well we're tireless, you and I, for we have far to go.

[*At a noise behind him, Raniero jumps up and whirls about, drawing his sword.*] Who is there?

[*Whirls again, finds himself surrounded by a gang of mean and ragged robbers. They rush in with shouts, brandishing their weapons. One overturns the candle. Raniero drops his sword and rescues the candle. He holds his right hand up.*]

Peace! For a moment I forgot myself. I am bound by a holy vow and will do you no harm. Take what you will – only leave me my candles – this one, and the two bundles tied on the horse.

[*The Robbers fall back a moment, amazed, but quickly recover.*]

1ST ROBBER:	Today I get the horse! And a nice piece of flesh he is! [*Exit*]
2ND ROBBER:	Here is his gold – a heavy pouch!
3RD ROBBER:	I get his sword!
4TH ROBBER:	I fancy your fine clothes. Undress, Sir!
RANIERO: [*Sets his candle down and takes off his mantle*] A moment, Friend. I must remove the Cross. [*Rips the cross off and hands the mantle to the Robber*]
	[*1st Robber enters again.*]
1ST ROBBER:	Here are your precious candles, crazy man. Go build yourself a bonfire! [*Robbers laugh.*]

CURTAIN

SCENE 3

Same as Scene 2. The squire comes on stage and points to the map, indicating a spot a day's distance from Ramle. The rock pile has been moved to the far right of the stage and changed.

[*Raniero comes on stage, sets his candle down behind the rock pile, seats himself and peers into the distance offstage left, as if looking into the sun. Sounds of an approaching caravan*]

RANIERO:	Here winds the dusty crew! A day's trip out of Ramle, I should guess! Pilgrims, troops, merchants, their beasts loaded with provisions. From their high spirits, it's not hard to guess the word has spread. Jerusalem has fallen, and they're hurrying there to worship – or to make a fortune. [*The group comes on stage, many pointing at him and shouting.*]
MOB:	*Pazzo! Pazzo!* Madman! Madman!
	[*Raniero springs up in anger and begins raining blows on the shouters. The mob cringes and runs off, except for two pilgrims who remain behind and offer Raniero a chunk of bread before they leave.*]
RANIERO:	*Grazie!* [*Watches them leave*] When will I learn to curb my temper? My countrymen were right to call me madman, the

kinder ones, to give me alms. No doubt they'd seen me cross the valley, riding backwards on a robber's nag. My vows of peace with men so soon are broken!

[*Looks around, gripped with sudden horror*] The candle! Is all lost? [*Looks behind rock pile*] My candle cold, and fire nibbling at the grass! No need to tramp it out. It can't burn far. [*Sits down with head in hands*] All is in vain! My candle's cold, its fire nibbles…its fire lives! [*Jumps up, picks up candle and runs off. Returns, cradling the lit candle in his hands. Sits on rock and addresses candle*]

Beloved Flame, who hast become more dear than life! Thy fragile golden glimmer – why does it move me so – like a shimmer, like a voice out of the past? I know, it was my wife. She tended a golden glowing love with faithful heart, while I forever blew ill-tempered winds that in the end snuffed out its tender light. If I could make amends? But nay, one deed, one dream remains for me to do. Thou Holy Flame I bear, must live to light the candle of my promise. Nor heartless deed, nor thoughtless breath e'er blow thee out, to plunge the world in darkness and in doubt!

CURTAIN

SCENE 4

Similar setting, this time with rock pile to the left. Squire indicates another span of the journey.

[*Enter Raniero, carrying a saddle in one hand, a candle in the other. He sets down the saddle.*]

RANIERO:
I can not go another league without a bit of rest – my wretched nag as well! [*Looking toward his horse offstage*] Indeed, I wonder, will that old bag of bones survive? A long and weary road lies yet ahead. [*Looks offstage in the opposite direction*] A ragged mad man's safer than a well-garbed knight. And yet the knot of pilgrims camping yonder with their fire gives me comfort.

[*Addresses candle as he sets it down beside a rock*] Here thou art protected from the wind. If I sit thus, [*half lies, leaning against rock*] this jagged rock will guarantee I sleep not long. [*Rises up again*] Shall I spare a fresh candle and make doubly sure?

[*Lights new candle and sets it in place. Lies down and sleeps. In his sleep moves and knocks over the candle, but doesn't wake. A Pilgrim comes quickly and takes candle away. At dawn Raniero awakes and searches for the candle but does not find it. Shrugs with feigned indifference*]

RANIERO: Ah well, the wise fool will admit his folly. I made one empty boast too many, when I undertook this hapless mission. But now it's over. Raniero must face failure, too. [*Shakes head sadly, unable to convince himself*]

1ST PILGRIM: [*Appears behind Raniero*] God greet you this fair morning, Friend! I hope the Angels blessed your sleep, despite the hardness of your pillow. I've brought a cup of soup, such as it is. 'Twill lend you strength to start the day.

RANIERO: God bless you for your kindness! [*Drinks*]

1ST PILGRIM: You will be looking for your candle. My brother brings it soon. He saved it when you knocked it over in your sleep.

[*Enter 2nd Pilgrim. Hands candle to Raniero*]

RANIERO: [*Without enthusiasm*] You Pilgrims are most kind. You've even troubled to light my candle afresh, despite the glow of dawn.

2ND PILGRIM: [*After brief pause – gently*] Do you not see how short the stub is? The candle never died.

RANIERO: But how?

2ND PILGRIM: We noticed when you camped, how carefully you prized this little flame, as though it were your very life. My brother and I have taken turns all night, to watch its fire and keep it safe for you.
[*Raniero looks unbelievingly at the Pilgrim.*]

1ST PILGRIM: Indeed, whatever is the secret hidden in your flame, it is unharmed.
[*Raises hand in gesture of blessing*]

BOTH PILGRIMS: God be with you, Friend!
[*Exeunt*]

RANIERO: [*Returning gesture*] God be with you! [*Falls to his knees and bows his head over the flame*]
CURTAIN

Same scene as before. Squire indicates that Raniero has reached Italy and is not far from Florence.

[*Enter Raniero, limping and walking backwards, sheltering his candle. Every other step he looks over his shoulder to sight his course.*]

RANIERO: Would that I had my faithful nag! She at least could see where we were going, while I must walk backwards into the wind. Ah well, I feel at last the beloved rock of my own land under my feet.
[*Turns around, sheltering his candle with a corner of his ragged cloak and stops*]
Below, a wide free valley stretches, glowing under the winter sunset. Florence and my journey's end lie hardly farther than yon hills. Why does my heart not sing then? Can it be I've come to cherish nothing but this small candle – the outer flame I hold in my hands? [*Softly*] And the inner flame I've never known before.

[*Enter poor woman with an unlit lamp*]

WIDOW: *Per favore, Signor!* Lend me a flame for my fire!

RANIERO: [*Drawing back*] Not from *this* candle! You must seek farther.

WIDOW: I've bread to bake at dawn for my hungry children, and nothing to light the oven!

RANIERO: I myself have shivered in winter chill more bitter than this evening's, rather than light from this candle a fire to warm me. The flame I guard is holy. I can not lend it.

WIDOW: [*Softly*] The flame I tend is sacred too – my children's lives that God has given unto my care. My children hunger and are alone in yonder cottage. We are far from neighbors and they will be afraid if night comes on.

RANIERO: You speak a truth. Here, take my light.

WIDOW: God bless you, friend! [*Exit*]

RANIERO: [*Thoughtfully*] The Fool said he would help widows and care for the sick – it's time he began. But who comes winding up this lonely hill?

[*Enter group of Peasants*]

1ST PEASANT:	Have we something to give this poor pilgrim? He looks most faint from hunger.
2ND PEASANT:	Our food is gone. We are so near to home. But he is cold in this spring chill.
3RD PEASANT:	Here, fellow, take my mantle. It's none so fine, but warmer than yours. I'll soon be home by the fire.

[*Throws mantle at Raniero. It falls over the candle and extinguishes it. Raniero looks in dismay at the candle, without a word or look of gratitude.*]

1ST PEASANT:	Ungrateful fellow.
2ND PEASANT:	He must be mad.

[*Exeunt Peasants. Raniero still stands dejectedly but then suddenly comes to life.*]

RANIERO:	The woman in her cottage! My flame still lives. She will return its fire. [*Hastens off*]

CURTAIN

ACT III

SCENE 1
Same scene as Act I, Scene 5, street with backdrop of painted houses.

[*Enter Gabriella and Ginevra, stage left, gossiping quietly. They are dressed for church.*]

GABRIELLA: [*Pointing*] There she comes!

GINEVRA: Is that Francesca on her balcony?

[*Enter Lucia, stage right, turning to wave to someone behind her. The others wave too.*]

GABRIELLA AND GINEVRA: *Bon giorno*, Lucia!

GINEVRA: We were coming to see if you would go to Mass with us.

LUCIA:	I stopped for Francesca, but she is waiting for her father.
GABRIELLA:	How is she?
LUCIA:	The same – patient, sweet –
GINEVRA:	And pale.
GABRIELLA:	She will never forget Raniero.

[*Disturbance in the distance, stage left, comes closer. It is possible to distinguish the cry, "Pazzo! Pazzo!"*]

LUCIA: [*Frowning*]	Whom are the urchins plaguing now?
GINEVRA:	A beggar fellow.
GABRIELLA:	How odd! He's walking backwards!
LUCIA:	Look! He is carrying a candle!
GABRIELLA:	He must be mad!

[*The crowd comes on stage. One urchin snatches off Raniero's mantle, revealing him in rags. Some of the urchins throw their caps at the candle, shouting, "Pazzo! Pazzo!" One jumps on another's back, puffs out his cheeks and tries to blow the candle out. Raniero holds his candle high over his head, disappears stage right, still surrounded by urchins.*]

LUCIA:	See how thin he is!
GINEVRA:	And ragged!
GABRIELLA:	Look, he's falling!
GENEVRA:	[*Excitedly*] Did you see? Francesca leaned down from her balcony and snatched the candle as he fell!
LUCIA:	Watch out! The urchins come this way again! [*The three girls hurry off stage left. The urchins return, laughing. One of them wraps himself ceremoniously in Raniero's mantle. All exeunt, stage left.*]

CURTAIN

The curtain rises again almost immediately. The scene is the same.

[*Raniero lies in a heap, motionless. Francesca comes running to him, carrying the golden cloth. She does not indicate that she has recognized him.*]

FRANCESCA: *Signor!* Are you all right? [*Bends over him, touching his shoulder, but he does not move. Carefully she covers him with the golden cloth.*] *Signor!* Here is your candle! I saw how intent you were to keep it burning, so I did not let it die.

RANIERO: [*Opening his eyes and fixing them on the candle*] The Sacred Flame from my Lord's Tomb! It lives! I must carry it to the Duomo! [*Grasping the candle, he laboriously climbs to his feet, the gold cloth sliding from his shoulders.*]

FRANCESCA: I'll go with you. I'm on my way to Mass. [*Steadies Raniero, walking slowly at his elbow*]

CURTAIN

SCENE 3
Inside the Duomo

[*Mass is in progress. Perhaps the muffled chanting of the Priest is heard offstage. The congregation is on benches, facing stage right, with an aisle between and open space behind. At stage left, visible on the far side are Jacopo and Taddeo, the Weavers, Oddo, Ginevra and Gabriella. On the near side are Renata, Lucia and Teresa with her husband and two children, a boy and a girl. The small girl leans in front of her brother to whisper to her mother.*]

SMALL GIRL: *Mama mia,* why aren't the candles lit?

TERESA: Because it's Easter Eve. Shhhh!

[*Enter Francesca. She genuflects and kneels beside her father.*]

SMALL GIRL: Why did the priest come in and whisper to the Bishop?

RENATA: Shhhh! I don't know.

[*Chanting stops. Priest comes into view at center aisle, stage right.*]

PRIEST: My children, it is a great day in Florence! Raniero di Raniero has come from Jerusalem, bringing a Sacred Flame lit at our Lord's

Holy Sepulcher. Many months he has traveled and many hardships endured. You will hear his story in the days to come. But today, Florence is proud of her son, whom our Gracious Lord has favored. Today Raniero will light the altar candles with his Holy Flame. Long may it burn!

[*A disturbance at stage left causes people to turn their heads. A Bishop, a Priest and Raniero with his candle enter. Oddo rises from his bench and goes toward them.*]

ODDO: Your Excellency, it is a great honor to Florence to receive such a Holy Fire. Such a thing has never happened to any city heretofore. But it is a long and perilous journey from Jerusalem. I'd like to ask how such a tender thing as a candle flame could have been borne so far. Must we believe this tiny flame never once went out in the wind or water? Is this whole wonder then to rest on one man's word?

PIERO: Perhaps he had a page with him, who now can testify?

RANIERO: God help me! How can I produce witnesses? I have made the journey alone. Deserts and mountain wastes must come to testify for me!

BISHOP: Raniero is an honest knight. We take him at his word.

FRANCESCA: [*Rushing up*] Yes, all the women in Florence will swear he speaks the truth!

ALFREDO: Not so the men. Raniero himself must know there will be doubts.

RICARDO: Indeed, he should not light the altar's candle with his flame until he offers proof of his wild tale.

WEAVERS: Hear! Hear!

[*Jacopo and Taddeo come out into the aisle.*]

JACOPO: All here know well how little friendship there has been between Raniero and me. Yet I believe him now. His aspect shows he is a changed and chastened man. My son and I, we will uphold him.

[*It looks as though a fight might develop. Raniero holds the candle high, a look of despair on his face.*]

SMALL GIRL:	Look, *Mama mia*, there's a sparrow in the church!
SMALL BOY:	Look! Look! It flew into the candle's flame!
SMALL GIRL:	And put it out! Look, the poor little bird's on fire!

[*All heads turn together as the bird circles.*]

TADDEO:	It's fallen dead on the Madonna's altar!

[*Raniero rushes forward with his candle and lights it from the burning bird feathers. The Bishop quickly follows, stopping where the audience can still see him and raises his hand.*]

BISHOP:	God has willed it, my son. You may light the candles with your fire. God has sent his sparrow to testify!
VOICES:	A miracle, a miracle! God has testified for him.

[*People quiet as the Bishop raises his hand again.*]

BISHOP:	May God send Florence many bearers of Eternal Light, that she become a city extolled among cities. May each of us in turn guard and cherish in his heart this Sacred Flame!
ALL IN CHORUS:	Let never heartless deed nor thoughtless breath Be brought to snuff the light, Engulfing the world in darkness and in doubt! But let it shine eternally in human hearts, Defended by valiant deeds, to light our ways.

CURTAIN

COLUMBUS

By Georg Starke
Translated by Barbara Betteridge

CAST

PRIOR
DOCTOR
MONK
COLUMBUS
DIEGO
SERVANT
KING
QUEEN
FIRST COURT LADY
SECOND COURT LADY
CHANCELLOR OF THE EXCHEQUER
COUNCILLOR
MINISTER
ADMIRAL
SAILORS: THE OLD ONE, THE TALL ONE, THE SHORT ONE, THE
    SLOW ONE, THE DOUBTER, THE YOUNG ONE, THE WATCH
FIGURES: THE PALE ONE, THE FIERY ONE
CHRISTOPHORUS
CHIEFTAIN
WARRIORS
PRIEST
TWO NATIVE WOMEN
NATIVE GIRL
OFFICER
THREE SAILORS
THREE NOBLEMEN
TWO WOMEN
DAUGHTER
KEEPER
COLON

SCENE I

A Monastery in Spain

[*Monks singing a vesper song heard in the distance. Enter Prior and Doctor.*]

PRIOR: What news, good Doctor, bring you from the world?
                      How fares the Court? The contest with the Moors?

DOCTOR: Your Reverence, you never will renounce
                      The time, long since, when you were at the Court.
                      I seek the quiet of these ancient walls,
                      And distance from the busy stir beyond,
                      While you persist in asking for the news!

PRIOR: It is our very breath of life, good Doctor.
                      I hold it an offense against the Lord
                      When one neglects to open heart and mind
                      Toward everything that happens in the world.
                      Be seated, please! A drink of fresh white wine
                      From our own vineyard will not come amiss!

DOCTOR: My thanks! — As ever, it is excellent!

PRIOR: I would remind you of our conversation
                      That time you spent some days with us before.
                      In speaking of the earth, and — yes — the stars,
                      You took exception to the old traditions
                      It long has been our usage to defend.
                       I can't conceive it! — But of that, anon —
                      My old-time friendship with the Queen demands
                      I ask at first, what's happening at Court?

DOCTOR: The newest's quickly told, Your Reverence.
                      The final bulwark of the hated foes
                      Of true belief, their fortress at Granada
                      Is ripe for siege. There's no doubt it will fall.
                      Already we're assembling at their gates;
                      It waits but for the drama to unfold.

PRIOR: Praise be to God! Then will the King again
                      Be free to dedicate his hands and strength
                      To full pursuit of his old goal: to win
                      The Holy Land once more to Christian faith.

MONK: [Entering quietly]

> I beg your pardon, Reverence. Outside
> There stand a pilgrim and his son.
> He asks for hospitality. And, too,
> It seems he has the wish to speak with you.

PRIOR:

> They are most welcome. See you bring them in,
> And give the boy at once whate'er he needs.
> [Exit Monk]
> [To the Doctor]
> Excuse the interruption!

DOCTOR:

> Your Reverence,
> 'Tis possible the stranger's traveled far
> And can contribute something valuable
> To the very matter you and I discussed.

COLUMBUS: [Enters with the boy, led by a monk]

> Your Reverence, forgive my bold intrusion
> If I disturb your peaceful evening hour.
> But we have traveled far to find you here.

PRIOR: [Regarding the two with sympathy]

> With all my heart, I bid you welcome, Sir!
> Here is a bench – another for the boy.
> Enjoy our hospitality, I pray,
> And tell me if there's anything you need.
> [To the Monk]
> Prepare some victuals, Brother, and a bed.
> [Exit Monk]
> Now tell us of your journey, and what goals
> Have brought you questing to our cloister door.

COLUMBUS:

> My name is Christopher Columbus.

PRIOR:

> Your name alone shows much significance.
> "The bearer of the Christ" the first part means;
> Then "Dove" or "Messenger of Holy Spirit."
> Indeed the image is a lofty one.

DOCTOR:

> Are you a scholar, as your name suggests?

COLUMBUS:

> No scholar, but a mariner am I.
> My home is Genoa, in Italy.
> Many a captain proud, my family boasts,

And early did I heed the ocean's call,
That's led me since on many a fateful voyage.
The craft of helmsman have I learned meanwhile.
And have applied myself to earnest study
Of geography, of all that's known,
Or guessed, or told, of Earth and sky and sea.
And most – of lands unknown beyond the sea,
From this, quite new ideas arose, and plans
I long with all my heart to carry out.
If only means there were at my disposal!
I find it easier from rigid rock
To strike to life a flowing spring of water
Than in just one hard head, full of tradition,
To make a crack for one unusual thought!
From court to court I wander, each entreat,
But none will see the possibilities
I offer, nor give me any hope of help.

DIEGO: Father, you *will* find help in the end, I know.
                 – But we are guests and in a stranger's house.
                 [*To the Prior*]
                 Diego is my name, Your Reverence.
                 Since Mother died, my father takes me with him.
                 Don't take it ill of him, I pray. He gets
                 Excited when he talks about his plans.
                 When you have heard them, you will understand,
                 For he is right, my father.

PRIOR: Good boy, Diego.
                 It's proper for a lad to defend his father.

MONK: [*Enters with a tray*]
                 A bite to eat. And pallets are prepared.

COLUMBUS: I thank you for your kindness! One request:
                 The boy is tired. May he go to bed?

PRIOR: Come, Diego. Take some fruit along.
                 The Brother will help you to your well-earned rest.

DIEGO: I thank you, sir, and bid you all good night.

COLUMBUS: Goodnight, my son. Be happy in your dreams!

[*The Prior accompanies Diego with the Monk to the door. Columbus, meanwhile, picks up an orange, but instead of cutting it, he turns it in his hand, looking at it thoughtfully. The Doctor and then the Prior watch him with some amazement.*]

COLUMBUS: [*To himself*]
It must succeed! My reckoning is right.
I've proved it many a time. The route is certain,
And shorter than the ones we follow now.
The very winds are even favorable!
[*He lays the orange on the table.*]
I fail to understand why all oppose me,
When such treasures beckon as reward!
[*To the others, as he comes out of his reverie*]
Forgive me!

PRIOR:
Apology's not needed. Still,
Your words and gestures offer many a riddle.

DOCTOR:
I have the feeling that Columbus brings
A contribution to our conversation.
What is the voyage you would undertake,
Whose prospects animate you so? Explain!

PRIOR:
Perhaps we should first say that when you came
We were discussing whether the earth is round
The doctor is a friend of this new thinking,
Although as yet I'm not in full accord.

DOCTOR:
You think this route will prove a shorter one?

COLUMBUS:
This, Toscanelli's map most clearly shows.
And he has made most careful reckonings
By every scientific means we have.
O, sirs, if you could only know what hope
This moment has awakened in my soul!
Imagine once, this orange to be the earth.

PRIOR:
You share the view then, that the earth's a sphere?

COLUMBUS:
Indeed I do! How could one *not*, who has
Exactly studied all the maps of Earth?
The Greeks had this opinion long ago.
And Toscanelli's proven it is true
With his new map. See! Here's the route
We usually travel toward the East,

If we would go to India. And yet
The land by no means comes to end there.
Beyond, of course, there is the great Khan's realm,
And further yet, the Island of Zipangu
That Marco Polo pictured as so rich,
The palace of its king was roofed with gold.
It stands to reason we would find these lands
If we should follow toward the *west* the sun.

PRIOR: A trip indeed with many dangers fraught!
For who would sail across such unknown waters?
Who knows the winds in all this watery waste,
And if the stars would show the selfsame aspects?

DOCTOR: One could assume that islands here and there
Might form a bridge before the continent.
Till now, there's nothing known of these. But think!
If they are there, 'twere well they were discovered.

COLUMBUS: I've also thought that through, a hundred times.
If there were such a bridge, we'd know of it.
Beyond the Canaries lies nothing but the ocean.
But courage is the tool to conquer that.
If the stars don't help us, there's the compass,
Whose needle holds unerring toward the north.
In this and in the sun we well may trust.
The wind's direction I have, through many reports,
And also scientifically tested.
This, too, well favors the adventure.

PRIOR: The purport of your speech is most incredible!
Yet as you tell it, the theory persuades.

DOCTOR: Advise us roughly what you estimate
Is needed to make the venture a success!

COLUMBUS: Three sturdy ships would well suffice our need,
Courageous men to man them, and supplies.
The money called for, though, is but a trifle,
When you consider the enormous wealth
That would result from a successful outcome.

DOCTOR: You're right! Whatever country should decide
To undertake with you the enterprise —
It will command the sea, the lands, the treasures,
Whatever you should find at journey's end!

COLUMBUS: According to reports that reach us here,
             There'd be rare spices and exotic fruit –
             Above all, gold. That would alone repay
             The cost of the adventure a hundredfold.

PRIOR: To which countries have you up to now
             Exposed your plans? You gave us the impression
             Your hopes had been rejected more than once.

COLUMBUS: The Portuguese, the Spanish, have declined.
             Each one is greedy for possessions, power –
             Yet none is willing to assume a risk.
             I have decided next to turn to France.

DOCTOR: It seems to me a great mistake for Spain
             To let this opportunity escape!
             Your Reverence, the Queen's a friend of yours.
             To progress she is favorably disposed.
             If you would give this man a reference,
             He could address his plea to her in person,
             And she the King could surely then persuade.
             Ah, what a glory you could bring to Spain!

COLUMBUS: It was with this hope, I confess, I've come.
             The many ministers shut off my access
             To the King – and he must needs approve.

PRIOR: I am convinced that these bold plans bode well
             For Spain, and will increase her rightful glory.
             The reference you ask I'll give you gladly,
             And urge you strike now while the iron is hot.
             The moment war in ended in Granada
             Will be the best to seek the King's good will.
             We'll keep the boy meanwhile and treat him well.
             But something yet lies on my heart, my friends.
             We've spoken of the treasures such a deed
             Can bring. We've talked of gold. We've talked of power.
             Invidious danger lies in each of these.
             We must be sure to ask ourselves as well
             What gifts we have to offer yon strange lands.
             Christopher Columbus is your name.
             You bear it proudly. Bear with it that world
             Which seems to me lies hidden in its meaning.
             Christopher Columbus, God bless your deed!

                        CURTAIN

SCENE II
The King's tent before Granada

[*The tent is empty. A Servant ushers Columbus and the Doctor in.*]

SERVANT: Their Majesties will soon assemble here
                 In this great tent, together with the Council.
                 Please wait outside this entrance till you're summoned.

DOCTOR: Columbus, I am convinced your hour has struck.

COLUMBUS: I thank you, Doctor, for your firm support.
                 What's good and right must in the end succeed.

DOCTOR: I wish you all good fortune in this hour.

                 [*Exeunt both*]

                 [*The Court enters with pomp from the opposite side. Their Majesties
                 are seated, the Councillors on the King's right, court ladies on the
                 Queen's left, their retinues behind and at their sides.*]

KING: It is my joy and honor, Your Majesty,
                 To lay the victory before your feet.
                 We will appropriately celebrate.
                 The people and the foreign states as well
                 Shall see Spain's might in fullest triumph reigning.

QUEEN: I'm honored by your words, Your Majesty.
                 Indeed I see Spain's power freshly blossom
                 Since our two noble houses are united;
                 And further triumphs surely are to come.
                 I beg you now, in front of other matters,
                 To heed to one request: Give audience
                 To the Genoese who waits outside. I mean
                 The man who offers such a rare proposal
                 To explore the ocean toward the setting sun.

KING: This man's a nuisance. But in spite of that,
                 I've ordered that his plan should be researched.
                 It's bold indeed — and yet, it's credible.
                 I'd welcome your opinion on the matter.

QUEEN: I must confess, the man doth please me well.

I wonder if his plan is so fantastic.
Our coffers are deflated by the war.
If he succeeds, new sources would be open
That could enrich the Crown. And on the seas,
Spain's power would command increased respect.
If we don't help him, others will. The fame
Of being first – this should be claimed by Spain.

KING: Let Christopher Columbus then be summoned!

[*Servant leads Columbus in.*]

SERVANT: Christopher Columbus, of Genoa!

[*Columbus kneels before the Queen, bows to the King, and takes his place to the right.*]

1ST COURT LADY: Is that the man who's so much talked about?
I find him charming!

2ND COURT LADY: How full of courage he looks!
If I were not a woman, I'd go with him!

CHANCELLOR: This fantast! What funds will he expect from us?

COUNCILLOR: The thing is not so dumb. He'll bring some in.

KING: You are the man who promises such riches,
If we should help you carry out your scheme.
Unfold your plan, and tell us what you need.
This is the hour and place to reach decision.

COLUMBUS: I thank Your Royal Highness, Your Majesty,
For your permission to present my plan.
It is my firm intent to sail yon sea
From East to West, and thus prove once for all
That Earth's a sphere.

CHANCELLOR: [*Laughs*] If he falls off the edge
Of the ocean, how will he get back up again?

COLUMBUS: Three caravels will suit my needs, with crews,
And with provisions for three months at most.
For the voyage back, we shall be well supplied
By the lands I count to find across the sea.

KING:	What think you then, most worthy counselors?
MINISTER:	I have grave doubts. It stretches my belief! Why, he would sail across the rim of hell And there be swallowed up, with man and mouse!
CHANCELLOR:	If this could be, it's highly hazardous To risk our precious money in this scheme. The treasury is somewhat undernourished. And yet I'll bow to more experienced counsel. There's risk in any business. It just might be This is the venture that could fill our coffers.
COUNCILLOR:	When I consider the honor and fame of Spain, I have to recommend we help the man. For since we turned him down before, it's clear He is inclined to offer France his plan. We can't afford to let some other country Reap the great rewards success would bring.
KING:	And what is *your* opinion, Admiral? You are the one experienced at sea. What you as expert say – this will decide.
ADMIRAL:	The undertaking has been well thought through. I recommend it to Your Majesty. The Genoese has capability, Nor does he lack in scientific background. It is unfortunate he lacks a fleet To call his own. For he must take the risk Upon his shoulders. Just think. The scheme might fail. We'll all admit that this is possible. Our fleet might then become a laughingstock Among our neighbors. Columbus then must do The deed with help of Spain, not Spain with *his* help.
KING:	Your opinion bears great weight with me. Now, what are the demands?
COLUMBUS:	I first demand The title 'Admiral of the Ocean' – also, 'Vice-regent' – these titles to apply forthwith To all the islands, seas and continents I shall discover.

CHANCELLOR: [*Holding up a contract*] Furthermore, he asks
A tenth of all the precious metals found.
For this consideration he will share
The costs that may arise in later commerce.

ADMIRAL: And finally he asks the jurisdiction
Of all the new-won lands.

KING: That goes too far!

COUNCILLOR: I urge we come to no decision until
The terms shall be more carefully considered
And a contract drawn that would protect
The interests of the Crown.

MINISTER: I, too, urge prudence.
Mark my words! The Church will be indignant,
And the people. For if Your Majesties
Were to vouchsafe, besides your royal consent,
Gold, too, it would be taken for a blasphemy.

2ND COURT LADY: Look how the Genoese's anger kindles!
Annoyance makes him all the handsomer!
If I were but a man and dared to say
what's burning in my heart!

1ST COURT LADY: It's my opinion
That they should hearken better to the Queen.
Her feeling can be trusted when it comes
To what can bring advantage to our land.
The lords are elderly. They lack in courage.
I, too, must much admire the Genoese.

QUEEN: No one can say we've been impetuous.
(My wish is only not to overlook
What might in future benefit the Crown.)
We know opinions in the Church are varied,
Yet my impression from many a discussion
Is: the majority are quite inclined
To favor the new science. These will defend
The boldness of our action to the people.
And with them, there's nothing so successful
As success. My verdict is in favor.

COLUMBUS: I must in fairness warn Your Majesties
              That if this present contract is rejected,
              I'll offer France my plan without delay.

              [*King confers quietly with the Queen.*]

MINISTER: His speech is not a little presumptuous.
              He even dares put pressure on the King.

ADMIRAL: I caution you against offending him.
              It is a message from France that makes him bold.

COUNCILLOR: I urge a quick assent. If we delay,
              His high demands are like to multiply.

CHANCELLOR: God forbid! The important thing is gain.

KING: Enough of talking! For time is of the essence!
              And more important matters wait on us.
              Christopher Columbus, hear our answer!
              The Court is still divided in its views.
              The Queen is on your side. If we agree
              That we should put some ships at your disposal,
              'Twill be to her that you will be indebted.
              And you – seek out a crew of men, prepared
              To undertake so hazardous a journey.
              Be sparing of the money, which I'll ask
              The Chancellor to lend you from our coffers.
              When these are gone, no more will be forthcoming.
              However, do not think that hope of gain
              Is all that influences our decision.
              The first commission I hereby charge you with
              Is carrying the Faith to lands remote.
              For that which motivates the Queen is hope
              You'll bear the Cross to countries yet unknown
              And bring the news of Christ to heathen hordes.
              This is, we know, a Christian's foremost duty.
              I bind you to it with a holy oath.
              You are to Spain's Crown now subservient.
              I charge you, bear this constantly in mind.
              Your signing of the contract will ensure it.

COLUMBUS: I hereby seal it with my signature
              And stand united with the Crown of Spain.
              [*Signs*]

The world will one day thank the Crown of Spain –
Momentous is the choice made here today.
As Christian do I undertake the mission.
Your Majesties, [*bows*] your wishes will be mine.

CURTAIN

SCENE III
On the sea

[*To the left, part of a ship projects into the scene. Columbus, the Doctor, Sailors. It is the free watch, and the sailors are sitting on the deck, singing and busying themselves with small tasks.*]

[*Song*]

WATCH:	[*Calls from the mast*] Hallo, hey, land! Hallo, hey, land!
YOUNG ONE:	Did you year him? Land! He cried out: Land! Land! [*Clambers up to see better*]
ALL:	Land! Land! Where is any land?
OLD ONE:	Hey, fellow, say! Where see you land?
WATCH:	To port, about two miles away! I see a coast, and trees, and smoke!
TALL ONE:	A beach, and people? Do you see them too?
DOUBTER:	I give a minute to this hope.
SHORT ONE:	I only see a bank of fog.
OLD ONE:	You should sharpen your eyes before you shout. For you, too, hope will soon die out.
SLOW ONE:	Come, youngster, before you break your neck! He cries alarm over every speck.
TALL ONE:	There's nothing there but water and fishes, And all you see is your empty wishes.

155

DOUBTER:	Come, brothers, let's sing and forget the sea.
	We're going to sail to Eternity.
SHORT ONE:	[*Sings a song of the homeland. All join in chorus.*]
YOUNG ONE:	Leave off your song! For once keep still!
	It matters no more, what the heart will.
	I'd like to see again Spain's palms,
	And sing in church my favorite psalms.
SHORT ONE:	And turn around, forsooth, to stare
	At the pretty maidens sitting there!

[*Enter Columbus and Doctor, unnoticed by sailors.*]

TALL ONE:	I measured the distance we traveled today.
	The wind's so dull, it troubles me.
	I wonder, up there, if they know their way.
SLOW ONE:	If what the distance was reckoned to be
	Is right, by now we're far behind.
	I wonder, up there, what's on their mind.
DOUBTER:	There's something clear as mud afoot.
	Methinks the Captain's bluffing a bit.
YOUNG ONE:	When we left, he vowed the wind
	Would be our firm and faithful friend.
SLOW ONE:	The allotted time's already past,
	And still far-off the foreign coast.
	If in this spot we stick and stay,
	We'll never reach it anyway.
TALL ONE:	The ship were just as well a jail.
	Rather a storm than that wind should fail!
YOUNG ONE:	Out of a jail a sly man can slip –
	But only to fishes, out of a ship!
SHORT ONE:	We *have* to find the promised shore –
	There's little left of viands more.
TALL ONE:	Take care how you joke about that coast.
	You're like to be the first we'll roast.

OLD ONE: [*Who has been listening in silence, anxiously*]
        Youngsters, I know where he's taking us.
        All that talk of a sphere is ridiculous.
        There's no place to go from here, but *down*.
        And down to where, I can't answer, I own.
        My father –

SLOW ONE: Sharpen your ears, good men!
        He is warming up *that* old joke again.

YOUNG ONE: Let him jabber!

DOUBTER: Oh, keep still!

OLD ONE: My father, I vow, could still think well.
        He who sails to the world's very rim –
        I've heard it many a time from him –
        When he comes to the place where it goes straight down,
        The dragon will swallow him, boots, soul, and crown.
        When a ship goes down with all its men,
        Nor wind, nor sun can raise it again.
        You've seen the flying fishes' shimmer,
        And on the horizon the fiery glimmer?
        There's worse to come, I sadly fear.
        The turning point, it must be near.
        The fire's formed by the dragon's breath.
        And the fishes, they bode of certain death.
        Where will it push us, the next wind that blows?
        Into the dragon's vicious jaws!

SHORT ONE: He is only spinning a foolish tale,
        Such as men babble over their ale.
        Let us see what Columbus says.

DOUBTER: We don't need talk. What we need is a breeze.

OLD ONE: Whether the sea be smooth or rough,
        We ought to turn back. We've had enough.
        Suppose we refuse him. What would he do?

SLOW ONE: That will but make him more stubbornly hew
        To his purpose. He won't give up, my men;
        But he'd bring us before the law in Spain.

OLD ONE: We'll just say simply, we won't go on.

TALL ONE:	Enough! Go fetch the Captain, someone.
ALL:	We won't go on! We won't go on!
COLUMBUS:	What means this, men: We won't go on? Speak out and tell me what's all the commotion! Is something wrong with the ship or the ocean?
OLD ONE: [*To the Tall One*]	Stand forth and tell him to what we've come.
TALL ONE: [*Hesitantly*]	We think, O Sir, you should turn toward home. Tell us the truth: Will we ever reach land? It's nothing but reason, what we demand. For every wave, as we know right well Is driving us nearer the rim of hell. We want to go home. Don't think it ill. But we won't go farther. We've had our fill!
ALL: [*Murmuring*]	We won't go farther. We've had our fill!
DOCTOR:	Hearken ye, men, I say it clear: I'm convinced the new land is not far from here. And I'll vouch for it, too, that a wind will rise. So rest ye awhile, is what I advise. When the doldrums end, as you'll agree, Each man will need the strength of three. Leave Columbus in peace, and ease your sorrow. We'll speak together again tomorrow. If naught has changed, we'll take council then As to whether it's time to turn toward Spain.

[*The sailors hesitantly withdraw.*]

COLUMBUS:	Once again I have to thank you, Doctor. You found the proper word to allay their fears. Till tomorrow you've consoled them. But what will happen, If *then* the situation be unchanged? I well can understand their restlessness. I'm troubled by our reckoning myself, And scarcely dare to trust the fickle compass. You were at the meeting yesterday When the captains from the other ships spoke out, Declaring neither could guarantee his crew. The people all are anxious to return.

DOCTOR: Leave off such dreary thoughts, my good Columbus!
                 It would be sinful now to turn around.
                 Thus far has Destiny remained your friend;
                 It waits the proper hour to send a wind.
                 I feel a change of weather in my limbs.
                 It figures that the plants and bits of wood
                 We've fished up from the water stem from land.
                 It can't be far away. So go to rest.
                 Tomorrow we can pacify the crew.

COLUMBUS: Your good words are a comfort to me, Doctor,
                 And yet I cannot come to inner peace.
                 Leave me for this hour here alone,
                 To contemplate the stars. Perhaps in them
                 I'll find the answers to tormenting questions.
                 [*Exit Doctor. After a long silence, Columbus prays.*]
                 Dear God, alone Thou knowest
                 If in my inmost thoughts
                 I sin against Thee.
                 Thou knowest that all my plans
                 Would serve Thy fame alone,
                 And glorify Thy name.
                 I pray Thee for a sign, to point my way!

                 [*A storm blows up, and mighty waves batter against the ship. The Pale
                 One and the Fiery One appear on the sea. The voices of both and of
                 Christophorus are spoken by a Chorus behind the stage.*]

CHORUS: Columbus, we call to you!

ECHO: Columbus, we call to you!

CHRISTOPHORUS: Columbus, I call to you!

COLUMBUS: What wondrous shapes are rising there!
                 They echo the questions that torment me so.

PALE ONE: Do you seek gold?
                 He'll reap tenfold
                 Who serveth me.
                 Gold turns to power
                 In man's brief hour.
                 I'll help, you see!

FIERY ONE: Do you seek fame?

	He'll reap the same Who serveth me. They'll honor you, And envy, too! I'll help, you see!
CHRISTOPHORUS:	Christopher Columbus! I call to you!
PALE ONE:	Gold turns to power In man's brief hour!
FIERY ONE:	They'll honor you, And envy, too!
BOTH:	D'you see the land? The golden strand? Serve then us! Your promise lend! The wind we'll send! Hold fast to us!
COLUMBUS:	What shall I, shan't I do? Are these thoughts clear and true?
CHRISTOPHORUS:	Christopher Columbus, I call to you!
COLUMBUS:	*That* call is honest! *That* call is true! Away, false shapes, I conjure you!

[*In the background, Christopherus, bearing the Child, moves slowly over the water. He is in a bright light, and the storm is for the moment quiet.*]

CHRISTOPHORUS:	The call of the Child Rings out to thee! Thou bearest my name: Follow me!

[*The storm rises again.*]

PALE ONE:	Gold turns to power!
FIERY ONE:	They'll honor you!

BOTH: And envy, too!

COLUMBUS: Begone, you powers!
                         You storm, be still!
                         I bear the name:
                         Christophorus!
                         I will!

                         [*The apparitions disappear. The storm subsides. The sun rises.*]

WATCH: [*From the mast*] Hallo, hey, land! Hallo, hey, land!

COLUMBUS: [*In utmost peace*]
                         There lies the land. 'Tis no deception more.
                         In the glimmer of early dawn beckons the goal
                         After the storm-troubled night. Yea, Lord, I will!

DOCTOR: There's land, at last! Columbus, what good fortune!
                         Come, people, look! There's no more turning back!

SAILORS: Land! Look there, the land! Our hope's fulfilled!

YOUNG ONE: Now all our wishes will be satisfied!

TALL ONE: Forgive our doubts, my lord! Forget as well!

COLUMBUS: Rejoice with me, good friends, for in this hour
                         Life's given us anew. Let's thank the Lord,
                         Give praise to our Creator for His blessings
                         And His wisdom that wondrously has led us.

CURTAIN

SCENE IV
On a beach, with a view of the sea

[*Native women on the beach, busying themselves with nets*]

1ST WOMAN: The gods are gracious to us. Many fish
                         Were captured by our nets in the last catch.
                         Indeed the nets were ripped by their heavy burden,
                         And all the boats were loaded to the brim.

2ND WOMAN: The ocean got a large part back again.
                         We couldn't use so bounteous a blessing.

1ST WOMAN: In spite of much good fortune recently,
A dread foreboding often overtakes me,
As if some strange Unknown were threatening,
And no one knows if it be good or evil.

2ND WOMAN: The flight of sea gulls seems a little changed.
And something in the Sun is otherwise.
Mornings when he rises from the waters,
Something burns in him like bloody fire.
Evenings, too, a strange, pale glow enfolds him,
As though he hid himself with heavy veils.

GIRL: [*Rushing in*]
Mother, have you seen my father lately?
The priest wants him. He orders urgently
That all the men be called to gather here.
For in the sacrifice were wondrous signs,
So strange the priest himself knows not their meaning.
They could bring evil, or they could bring luck.

1ST WOMAN: The chieftain and the men are down the beach,
Busy readying the boats to go out fishing.

[*Exit Girl, running*]

2ND WOMAN: This message strangely follows on the heels
Of what we spoke together even now!

1ST WOMAN: Uncertainty in all the signs prevails,
I wonder what these omens may portend.

[*Priest enters.*]

PRIEST: Has your daughter already come this way?
I bade her summon the chief and all the men.

1ST WOMAN: Indeed, as with wings of a falcon she sped!
And see – they come!

[*Chieftain enters with natives.*]

CHIEFTAIN: The news did not astonish us.
We too have noticed signs both rare and strange,
And meant to ask you what you make of them.

PRIEST:
The scudding flight of clouds presages storm
From yonder where Father Sun is wont to rise –
Most unaccustomed for this time of year.
The picture of the sunrise was a strange one,
And rare birds swept in loops across the skies.

1ST WOMAN:
Ourselves have marked the same unusual views,
And yet felt nothing threatening therein.

2ND WOMAN:
What omens found you in the sacrifice?

PRIEST:
I could not read in the uncertain signs
Whether our fortunes should be good or ill.
I recommend perpetual sacrifice
To ensure the lasting favor of the gods.

CHIEFTAIN:
Call everyone to the place of sacrifice!
There we will duly seek to appease the gods.

[*A thunderclap sounds, with a long reverberation. Girl rushes in.*]

GIRL:
Father, the gods are coming here to us!
With long strides they glide across the water.
Higher than the palm trees tower their heads.
Wrapped in splendid robes of red and white,
They carry thunder and lightning in their hands.

CHIEFTAIN:
This is the riddle's answer. Up, ye women!
Hurry to the huts! Don festival attire!
Meanwhile, let us conceal ourselves for now,
Until we have looked over those who come,
That we may give them that reception due.
They may be gods. They could as well be foes.

[*Exeunt women. The men conceal themselves behind bushes.*]

1ST MAN:
I see three houses standing in the water.
So high and broad that only gods could build them!

2ND MAN:
Strange trees rise up from these, and hanging in them
Are creatures that in form resemble *us*.

1ST MAN:
The color of their skins is different.
A sort of white, but darkened, almost golden.

CHIEFTAIN: A little boat is leaving one great house.

1ST MAN: It's headed toward the island – toward this beach.

2ND MAN: We'd better have our weapons ready to use.

CHIEFTAIN: Hold fast your weapons till they have approached.
                    We must discover if they're friendly first,
                    Lest we provoke the anger of the gods.

1ST MAN: They have set foot on land, their chieftain first.

2ND MAN: Look! They bear a most remarkable tree!
                    It has no leaves at all, and only two branches
                    That stretch out toward the sides like arms.

CHIEFTAIN: Hide now,
                    And wait quietly until I give you a sign!

                    [*They withdraw to right and left toward the rear. Columbus enters
                    with the Doctor, officers and Sailors who are bearing a cross, the royal
                    banner of Spain and banners of the Green Cross (an emblem Columbus
                    had adopted as Admiral.) They kneel. Some kiss the ground, some
                    embrace each other in joy. Then Columbus rises solemnly.*]

COLUMBUS: New land, I greet thee! Hallowed be this ground
                    Whereon I first set foot! Let us give thanks
                    To our Creator; let us praise His name!
                    The very tide of time with this our journey
                    Turns. From this day forth, the world will change.
                    With new eyes all mankind will view that star
                    That is our habitation in the cosmos.
                    Let now the cross be planted in the ground!
                    I dedicate this new land to the Savior,
                    And christen it, for Him, San Salvador!
                    [*The sailors sing the "Te Deum."*]
                    After this sacred service, be it proclaimed:
                    In the name of Their Majesties, the King and Queen,
                    I take possession of this foreign land!
                    From this day forth, it shall belong to Spain!

OFFICER: [*To the Doctor*] I only hope we find sufficient gold
                    To fill Spain's empty coffers to overflowing.

DOCTOR:

That would naturally be the wish
You utter in this solemn, festive moment.

1ST SAILOR:

The Admiral and his words quite move the heart.

2ND SAILOR:

I must confess I'm near to tears myself.
I wonder what they'd say to this in Spain!

3RD SAILOR:

Have you noticed those strange fruits that hang
In such amazing branches? Can one eat them?

OFFICER:

It is odd that not a single human soul
Should stir to greet us on arrival. And yet
I seem to hear a rustling in the bushes.

[*Chieftain appears with other natives. The women enter carrying fruits and wreaths of flowers.*]

PRIEST:

Do you in peace approach our smiling shores?
Can you show proof of friendliness, great Chief,
And that you hide no evil in your hearts?

CHIEFTAIN:

[*Steps in front of Columbus*]
We come before you with respect, great Chief.
Strange to our ears have sounded the words from your lips.
Strange to our eyes is the color of your skin.
Strange to us as well are your ceremonies.
You come in boats as great as the gods' own houses.
You carry thunder and lightning in your hands
And erect before us mystifying signs.
If you be not gods yourselves, then tell us, pray,
The names of the gods who sent you to our shores.

OFFICERS:

His heathen gibberish is Greek to us,
His gestures seem to indicate submission.
But who can tell if the churl be not deceitful?

COLUMBUS:

Although our words ring strangely on your ears,
Your finer feeling will perceive their meaning.
Beyond the clouds, a mighty Chieftain rules
Whom every people on the Earth shall serve.
For He has conquered Evil in the world.
His symbol have you seen us here erect,
And in this sign we come upon your shores.

OFFICER: He ought to make, instead, some show of force.
This matter isn't done with pious talk.

DOCTOR: The way he has elected is the right one.
It will persuade them quickly of our friendship.

PRIEST: I think, my lord, you tell us of your gods.
We see they are indeed far more exalted
Than those we're wont to worship at our altars.
So teach us how to serve them, we beseech,
And we at once will make a sacrifice.

WOMEN: Clear is the meaning now of our dreams.
The times are changing. The new is born.

[*They begin to dance and sing, bestowing their flowers and fruits.*]

1ST SAILOR: Get an eyeful of that golden jewelry!
The sight of all those riches cheers the heart.

PRIEST: Dark grew the ancient sacrifice.
No more its sense we read.
Praise be the one who to us brought
A new one in its stead!

COLUMBUS: So trust responds in turn to offer of trust.
So lasting friendships here on Earth are woven,
When realms of gods encounter one another.
That friendship may work on, hear our pronouncement:

OFFICER: [*With document*]
Their Majesties, the King and Queen of Spain,
Hereby proclaim to all subordinate chieftains:
Whereas we take possession of your lands,
Columbus as our representative
Shall guarantee protection of your realm
From enemies and guard the rights of subjects.
In turn you are obliged to yield to him
Some token of your fealty, and treasures
Of the earth befitting the Crown of Spain!

CHIEFTAIN: Explain to us the meaning of your words.

COLUMBUS: This gold your women are wearing as jewelry—
Do you have more such stones here in your land?

	We seek some for our King because he needs it
	In order to protect you and your people.
CHIEFTAIN:	'Tis Sun's own gold we wear as decoration.
	We won it long ago as prize of war
	And gladly give it you as sign of friendship.

[*He removes his own adornments and offers them to Columbus. The warriors and women follow suit.*]

WARRIORS & WOMEN:	The Sun himself bestows the gold
	We give you: for friendship dear we hold.
	Within its glow the Sun doth shine.
	Oh, may it be true friendship's sign!
OFFICER:	They prate of friendship, these heathen braves?
	Why, they are nothing more than slaves!

[*Columbus sinks into a deep reverie.*]

PALE ONE: [*On the right side*]

> Gold will flower
> To wealth and power.
> The gleam of the sun –
> This you have won.
> I gave it to you!

FIERY ONE: [*On the left side*]

> Now you may claim
> Honor and fame.
> Wherever you go
> You'll bask in their glow.
> I gave them to you!

CHRISTOPHORUS: [*Voice from behind scene*]

> Christopher Columbus, think of me!

DOCTOR:	Wake up from your daydreams, Admiral!
	Have you not already attained your wishes?
	Perhaps you're looking back to bitter times.
	Look ahead! Yet farther shall you go!
COLUMBUS:	'Yea, Lord, I will!' These were my very words
	When Gold and Fame have sought before to tempt me

To betray the lodestar of my name.
Dimly I sense that gathered in this place
Are other Powers, bent on gain, most eager
To extend their dark dominion here.
Human beings they hold in base contempt.
Our friends could rot in chains, for all they care.
For the glory of One Higher, I set forth,
Who gave man freedom in the truest sense.
The land to which His guidance safely led me
I render unto Him, as His possession.
His right here shall prevail, I give my word.
So long as I shall live, His Name commands me.

[*Sailors sing the "Te Deum" once more.*]

CURTAIN

SCENE V

Prologue
In front of the curtain, before the cabin in which Columbus is

[*A street in the harbor city, dimly lit by a lantern on an inn, very late at night. In front of the tavern, a beggar is singing a ballad in a half-singing, half-speaking manner, accompanying himself on a guitar or other instrument.*]

BEGGAR: There sailed a man to sea,
                      Ah, me!
                 He sailed forever West
                 Beyond the Sun's own nest –
                      To sea! Ah, me!

                 To new lands would he come,
                      Not (so) dumb!
                 It seems he had in mind
                 Some treasures there to find –
                      At sea! Ah, me!

                 Not easy he to frighten,
                      This Titan!
                 Of gold he sought a sky-full
                 But found a paltry eyeful –
                      At sea! Ah, me!

168

Since people heard of that,
     Great hat!
Revenge they ask and such –
He'd promised oh so much –
     At sea! Ah, me!

In chains he now is stuck,
     Bad luck!
But though the people jail him,
Once more he'd like to sail him
     To sea! (Ah, me!) Huzza!

[*Enter two noblemen on their way home*]

1ST NOBLEMAN: Toss him a little coin to stop his noise!
I hear the fellow bawling every evening.
See him day-times loafing in the alleys.

2ND NOBLEMAN: He seems to know something he isn't telling.
Here, old one! Move along now – *muy pronto*!

[*Beggar disappears into the darkness.*]

1ST NOBLEMAN: During the day you must have heard the news:
Columbus has returned.

2ND NOBLEMAN: Indeed I did.
But I'm amazed how that old beggar has
The latest on his tongue. He often seems
To know more of a thing than those concerned.

1ST NOBLEMAN: It doesn't puzzle me. For I'm convinced
The fellow made the first trip with Columbus.
He still has threads that link him to his comrades.
Perhaps we should have listened to him better,
To find out what the Admiral conceals.

2ND NOBLEMAN: Already on the first trip, that Pinzon
Who had command of the second ship, the Pinta,
Became separated from the others –
He claims to have found gold in quantities.

1ST NOBLEMAN: We've hardly seen a glint or hint of it!

2ND NOBLEMAN:	Indeed! And where could it be hiding? The crew Has not returned home rich from their adventure.
1ST NOBLEMAN:	The thing has only brought us sacrifice. That should long since have yielded up a profit.
2ND NOBLEMAN:	This last one was already the third trip.
1ST NOBLEMAN:	There's something very much amiss in all. There should have been a greater supervision. First was Columbus gentle, then severe. When he failed to find more gold, he took The people whom he'd offered the hand of friendship.
2ND NOBLEMAN:	And now sent them over here to Spain as slaves! In that, he sharply did offend the Queen, Who holds the rights of human beings holy.
1ST NOBLEMAN:	Then Bobadilla was sent over there To take upon himself the governing. Through him perhaps the gold will flow our way. He's been most harsh toward the Admiral And finally committed him to chains.
2ND NOBLEMAN:	So it is true, what I would not believe? Columbus is enchained upon the ship?
1ST NOBLEMAN:	[Coldly] Yes. And in my view, it serves him right! [Third nobleman enters out of the shadows.]
3RD NOBLEMAN:	Psst! I heard you speaking of the latest Gossip, that's rocked the city all day long. If it's true Columbus is in chains, 'Twere best not openly to jubilate. He still had many friends here in this land.
1ST NOBLEMAN:	Who will desert him when the truth comes out.
3RD NOBLEMAN:	Just wait, my friend, until you've ascertained The viewpoint of the King and Queen toward this. They hold Columbus still in high regard.
2ND NOBLEMAN:	'Tis my opinion, injustice has been done him.

1ST NOBLEMAN:	Let us not put our necks in the noose for him –
	At least until we have assured ourselves
	He has enough influence left to make it pay,
	Lest it befall –
3RD NOBLEMAN:	Desist! We're overheard!

[*Exeunt all three*]

[*Beggar comes out of the shadows and sings, rather soflty the third and fourth stanzas of the earlier song.*]

[*Enter three Sailors in high spirits*]

1ST SAILOR:	Sing on, gaffer, you do us cheer!
2ND SAILOR:	Your song should *all* the people hear!
3RD SAILOR:	Even those who've gone to bed
	should hearken to your chant instead!

[*All start to bawl the third stanza.*]

1ST SAILOR:	Say, have you heard, Columbus' ship
	Foundered once upon a reef?
2ND SAILOR:	Younker, that was a storm to see!
	The wind did roar so horribly.
	It blew your words back onto your teeth!
	The old one, it robbed of every breath!
3RD SAILOR:	For that, the Admiral's not to blame.
	We live; we've no excuse to complain.
1ST SAILOR:	He'd little patience, as people say,
	But always wanted to have his way.
	Go on and on…
2ND SAILOR:	But he was right!
	That is what you seem to forget.
3RD SAILOR:	Long live Columbus! He's the man
	Who everything can –
ALL:	Yea, he's our man!

[Enter two women, the first, an innkeeper]

1ST WOMAN: In the name of goodness, hold your row!
You'll never save Columbus so.

1ST SAILOR: I've heard no mention here of saving.
What goes?

2ND SAILOR: The woman must be raving.

2ND WOMAN: Can it be you haven't heard
They've brought Columbus home in chains?
For all his courage, this reward
He gets. Of glory, dust remains.

2ND SAILOR: In chains returns the Admiral,
Like any common criminal?
You must be mad!

1ST WOMAN: How would you know?
You sit all day there in the inn
And drink and sing and make a din –
But the world goes on, you must allow.

3RD SAILOR: Now the old man's song comes clear.

2ND SAILOR: Come, fellows, let's get out of here.
And seek the truth without delay!

1ST SAILOR: Would we long since were underway!

[Sailors hasten off. The two women remain. Enter girl, the innkeeper's daughter]

1ST WOMAN: All those proud deeds of yesterday! And what
Do they amount to now? A hill of beans!

DAUGHTER: No, Mother, no! How can you say such things?
Columbus is a great man, full of courage!
Proud and good is he.

1ST WOMAN: How would you know?
A child you were, and never saw him either.
DAUGHTER: You've told me many a wondrous tale of him.
So've others, too. I know him very well.

2ND WOMAN:	Not all the natives he brought back with him
	Came to our land as slaves. The first came free,
	A few have even studied to be priests,
	And these have always spoken well of him.

DAUGHTER:	And some of those they brought were children, too.
	I've talked with them, just as I talk with you.
	They were happy and indeed, seemed quite like us.
	They always spoke of Columbus as a father –
	And one whom you call Father, you must love.

1ST WOMAN:	We'd like to believe that you are right, my child.
	[To Second Woman]
	The first came free. What good is such fine freedom,
	When soon you learn you must submit to the stronger?

2ND WOMAN:	The stronger does not always mean the better.
	Between these walls we oft experience
	Such painful things. We too, do not feel free.
	If one could leave it all!

| 1ST WOMAN: | Quite so – and yet, |
| | We must feel grateful that these walls protect us. |

DAUGHTER:	[Quietly, to her mother]
	If I could only be a boy, dear Mother,
	I'd never have a greater wish than to follow
	Columbus to the ends of the earth. Imagine
	Being able to make such splendid plans –
	Then carry them out!

| 2ND WOMAN: | The chains won't hold him long. |

| 1ST WOMAN: | This we may wish for him – and pray for him. |
| | But we must go in the house. 'Tis very late. |

[Exeunt. Beggar comes out of the shadows and sings the last stanza of his song.]

CURTAIN

Cabin on a ship where Columbus is imprisoned

[*An intermediate curtain discloses the cabin. A table, two stools, a bed, and in front, the chain which the good Keeper has removed; above the table, a cabin lamp. Columbus, in a brown frock like that of a Franciscan friar, only shorter, is sitting on a stool with his head laid heavily on the table. Keeper knocks softly on the cabin door.*]

KEEPER:
Are you awake, sir?
[*Knocks again. Enters quietly*]
Someone has come to see you –
A young friend of yours. He'd speak with you.

COLUMBUS:
Who can it be?

KEEPER:
He's one of the foreigners
You brought here to our country, now long since.
Not one of those, however, who hates his lot.
He has wide-open eyes.

COLUMBUS:
That is Colon,
A fine young fellow. Do let him in at once!

[*Colon enters with a light step. Keeper leaves.*]

COLON:
O Father! This little room – and there are chains!
[*He turns away to hide his weeping.*]

COLUMBUS:
Come now. The chains have been removed already.
The good Keeper constantly bestirs himself
To do me some kind turn – though secretly.
But say: What brings you here at such a time?

COLON:
I looked for you. The rumor you are here
Doth run through every inn and alley, and stirs
Malicious tongues to wag at your expense.

COLUMBUS:
That *could* disturb one, but disturbs not me.
I've learned long since that fame and also riches
Are quickly fled.

COLON:
There's more to it, I know.
When first you landed on our little island,
'Twas your intent to bring us something new.
A cross stood there – quite simple – with no pretense,

Humble, and yet in majesty upright.
The cross demanded neither gold nor fame.

COLUMBUS: But I did – and my officers as well.

COLON: In our astonishment we failed to mark it;
For such a wonder, such a miracle
We felt, although we couldn't understand it.
It meant a new God came to us on earth.
And then you made us leave, and come to Spain.

COLUMBUS: Of course. 'Twas right for you to go to school here
And get to know our language and our customs.
Don't think it was betrayal of your brothers
That in the end you wished to serve the new Lord,
Of whom you felt that He could bring you good.
It was our thought that you could be a help
In strengthening the friendship of our lands,
When you'd become accustomed to Spain's ways.

COLON: But can you understand, it was not easy.
With everything at first so strange and new?
Then soon we noticed much that was not honest.
What was at first surprise became contempt.
You were not there. In whom could we then trust?

COLUMBUS: I had commissions still to carry out
And thought you'd be well cared for in my country.

COLON: And so it was. Yet rumors reached our ears
That you had changed, and soon our country folk
Began arriving here in chains – not free,
As we had been. Oh no! As slaves they came!
Oh speak, Columbus, whom we've called our father
And our friend. Was this at your command?
Oh, say it wasn't so!

COLUMBUS: It *was,* my friend.
I was not free to follow my own heart.
I was required to find gold and goods
To fill again my country's empty coffers.
The concept that the earth was like a ball,
Which first had spurred me on a westward trip,
Was proven now as truth. There was nothing left
But to plunder the lands we had discovered.

COLON:	You could, as Admiral, forbid such measures!

COLUMBUS:	Nay, my friend —things only seem that simple. The heavy chain that lies there by the bed Is lighter than the burden of commanding — And one's own greediness. 'Tis that slinks in To coil itself about one like a snake And make one covet ever more and more. How often to St. Francis have I prayed?

COLON:	He chose poverty – and became rich.

COLUMBUS:	And free within his soul.

[*Enter Keeper*]

KEEPER:	Hear me, sirs! I beg you earnestly to cease your talking. If anyone should hear you, it would bring you Punishment. And I should fare ill, too.

COLON:	I bid you for the nonce, farewell! Be sure That we, your friends, will find a way to free you – You whom we owe so much. O dearest Father, Whose pain we feel as though it were our own! Adios, my Father!

COLUMBUS:	My son, Adios!

[*Exeunt Keeper and Colon. Columbus seats himself on the bed or a stool.*]

> They call him Diego, my good friend who was here.
> Diego, like my son. How clearly I see
> Before me that evening in the cloister's hall,
> And hear the boy say, "Just have faith, my father,
> I know your plan will in the end succeed!"
> And has it then succeeded? Is there no more?
> We're masters of the lands and of the seas –
> The whole earth-ball will soon belong to us.
> But does that mean we're free? In those past days,
> Did I answer rightly to the call,
> "Christopher Columbus, follow your name?"

[*The near wall has divided. Christophorus appears in the center in a bright light. Columbus remains in half-darkness, in a kind of dream.*]

CHRISTOPHORUS: Christopher Columbus! Follow your name!
Christopher Columbus! Think of me!

COLUMBUS: That is the call that yet can bring new hope,
Like a beacon on a distant shore
That shines to save a ship that's lost its way.

CHRISTOPHORUS: The Earth is the Lord's, Christopher Columbus!
Do not forget the lodestar of your name,
For with you into life on earth it came.
"Yea, Lord I will!" 'Twas thus that you did speak
When once you felt your human worth was threatened.
You ask for freedom. In the right place, seek!
The human being, you yourself profaned.
Forgotten what you once upheld and praised –
The truth that he should not henceforth be chained.
Learn to love your fellow man. Unswerving,
Serve him all your life. Become a brother
To everyone who here on earth is serving.
Raise the Child upon your shoulders then.
You love St. Francis. He taught all men:
Possession gives one neither worth nor freedom.
'Twas for the glory of a Higher One
You once went forth. Afar you bore the Dove.
Now carry on what was so well begun.

COLUMBUS: [*Softly*]   And where I stray in error from my path?

CHRISTOPHORUS: Begin anew! To be a man – that means
To learn and to become. That gives life meaning.
And every moment is a new beginning!

COLUMBUS: If duties call, to which I am committed?
If earthly powers direct what way I go?
(If I am given freedom again at all.)

CHRISTOPHORUS: That is no freedom! I bid you, be awake!
In every choice, learn how to tell who speaks.
And when your path divides, and you're uncertain,
Call on me! I never will forsake you.

[*It becomes dark again. The apparition disappears. Day begins to
dawn. The Beggar is heard in the distance once more, singing the last
stanza of his song. As it dies away the Keeper knocks and enters.
Columbus rises.*]

KEEPER: Pardon, my Lord. A messenger has come
                     From the King. 'Tis passing strange at such an hour.

                     [*Officer enters and bows respectfully. He has in his hand an official order. As he speaks, Columbus stands erect showing no emotion and remains so until the curtain.*]

OFFICER: Your Excellency! Columbus! You are free!
                     Their Majesties, the King and Queen, hereby
                     Request that you attend them in the morning.

                     [*All remain standing still for a moment. In the background the apparition of Christophorus becomes momentarily visible.*]

CHRISTOPHORUS: [*Softly*] Christopher Columbus, think of me!...

                     [*The apparition disappears. For a moment there is complete silence. Then music begins and the Chorus begins to sing either the first stanza of the sailor's song or a sacred song. With the beginning of the music, the curtain gradually closes.*]

                              CURTAIN

_____

Scenes I through IV were written at Easter 1950 at Marburg/Lahn for the eighth grade graduation and were also performed in Krehfeld by the seventh grade. The fifth scene was added in November 1963. The play was performed by the eighth grades in Landschulheim Schloss Hamborn and in Pforzheim and translated and performed at Highland Hall in 1964 by permission of the author.

THE OTHER WISE MAN

Story by Henry Van Dyke
Dramatized by Barbara Betteridge

One night as Henry Van Dyke lay in pain and close to death, he "saw" this story of a fourth Wise Man enacted before his eyes. He carried the legend in his heart for many years and then he wrote it down, calling it The Story of the Other Wise Man. The original should be read as background for this play, as it presents not only the mood, but the settings and costumes as well.

CAST

ARTABAN
TIGRANES
ABDUS
ABGARUS
RHODASPES
BARDYA
HEBREW
ANNA
SIMON
CAPTAIN
INNKEEPER
PERSIAN GIRL
FIVE SOLDIERS
FOUR WOMEN
PASSERSBY

ACT I

ARTABAN: [*Receiving guests – six or more – into his home in Ecbatana, Persia*]
Tigranes, welcome! Abdus, peace be with you!
Rhodaspes, and you, my father Abgarus!
Your presence makes my house grow bright with joy!
[*Greets the others, leads them in*]
'Tis good of you to come at my behest.
Ahura-Mazda waits our evening worship.
When we have fed his flames I shall explain.
[*All gather around a small black altar, where a tiny flame is burning.
Artaban waves a barsom of tamarisk branches over the fire, feeding it*

179

with dry sticks of pine and fragrant oils. They chant a hymn to
Ahura-Mazda. Artaban then moves to the arched doorway, open to a
terrace, and speaks.]
The night is moonless, crystal clear and cool,
And from the farthest harbors of the sky
There shine the solemn portraits of the stars.
Look! Yonder over towering Zagros' crest,
Tonight, if I mistake not, will appear
A star that is not named in all our lore.
Will you await it with me?

TIGRANES: What nonsense this!

ABDUS: Preposterous!

ABGARUS: What prompts your words, my son?
                 Pray tells us, Artaban, what is your mind?

ARTABAN: Hear me then, my father and my friends!
                 We all are followers of Zoroaster,
                 And long we Parthians have sought to learn
                 The lore of earth and air, of water and of fire,
                 And yet, beyond all these, the mysteries
                 In starry script across the heavens flung.
                 Though much we know, there's more beyond our ken.

TIGRANES: And much beyond our ken will still remain.
                 The brilliant light of Zoroaster fades,
                 Yet what abides of wisdom must suffice us.

ABDUS: Our men are posted on the mountaintops
                 To wait a new sunrise. And yet we know,
                 Though Powers of Light with Darkness still contend,
                 They are predestined equal to remain.

ARTABAN: I do not share this view. For if in vain
                 We wait a new sunrise, then it is folly.
                 We would be like those teachers of the Greeks
                 Who say there is no truth, that wisdom rests
                 In recognizing lies that have been taught.
                 But I believe the new dawn will appear
                 At the appointed hour. Do not our books
                 Relate that this will surely come to pass,
                 And men shall see one day a great new light?

ABGARUS: You speak a weighty truth indeed, my son.
                  For every son of Zoroaster knows
                  This prophecy of the Avesta well
                  And carries deep within his heart this word:
                  "There shall arise among the prophets once
                  That Sosiosh who shall be greatest of them all.
                  Around him there shall shine a mighty brightness.
                  'Tis he shall bring to men life everlasting.
                  'Tis he shall raise the dead to life anew."

TIGRANES: This saying is a dark one to my mind
                  And best forgotten. It were far better
                  For us to concentrate on things at hand,
                  Extend the Magi's power, than look afar
                  For one who might to us a stranger be,
                  That we to him our power may resign.

                  [*All except Abgarus nod agreement.*]

ARTABAN: [To Abgarus] This prophecy yet deeply stirs my soul.
                  Religion without hope can only be
                  An altar where there burns no living fire.
                  For me the fire burns brightly. By its light
                  Have I read other words from Truth's own fount
                  That speak more clearly still of Him to come.
                  [*He draws from his tunic two small scrolls of fine linen and unrolls
                  them upon his knee.*]
                  Before our fathers came to Babylon
                  The wise men of Chaldea taught this lore
                  To whose who were the earliest of Magi.
                  Of all who learned the secrets of the stars
                  The mightiest was Balaam. Hear his word:
                  [*Reads*]
                  "Out of Jacob there shall come a star,
                  A scepter out of Israel arise."

ABDUS: [*Contemptuously*]   Judah was a slave in Babylon
                  And Jacob's sons in bondage to our kings.
                  The tribes of Israel are scattered sheep.
                  From those who in Judea bear Rome's yoke
                  Shall neither star nor kingly scepter rise.

ARTABAN: And yet it was the Hebrew Prophet Daniel,
                  Interpreter of dreams to mighty kings
                  And reader of the thoughts of God, who said:

[Reads from second scroll]
"Know ye therefore, hear and understand,
That from the going forth of the commandment
To restore Jerusalem, till He,
The Prince, the great Anointed One, shall come,
The time is seven and threescore and two weeks."

ABGARUS:

[Thoughtfully]
These numbers, though, my son, are mystical.

ARTABAN:

Most eminent of Magi are the three
From whom it was my privilege to learn
The starry wisdom: Melchior and Caspar,
Balthazar too, wise men of high repute.
The tablets of Chaldea we have searched
And reckoned out the time. It falls this year.
We've studied long the sky. And in the spring
This year we saw two of the greatest stars
Draw near together in the Fishes sign,
Which is the Hebrews' House. We also saw
A new star there that shone one night and vanished.
Once more the two great planets are conjoined.
Tonight in Babylonia the others
In the Temple of the Seven Spheres
Are keeping watch. And I am watching here.
If that star shines, they'll wait ten days for me.
It is our purpose to Jersusalem
To journey. For we intend, if God so wills,
To find and worship Him, the Promised One,
Who shall be born the King of Israel.
My house I've sold and my possessions all.
For these in turn three jewels have I bought
Of rarest worth.
[Draws them out of his girdle and shows them to the others]
A ruby like the rays
Of rising sun, a sapphire dark as night,
A pearl as pure as snow on mountain peaks.
These then will be my tribute to the King.
Will you go with me on this pilgrimage?
Shall we together seek the worthy Prince?

[His friends glance at each other with looks of wonder and pity, like those who have listened to the story of a wild vision.]

TIGRANES:

Believe me, Artaban, your dreams are vain.

It comes from too much looking at the stars.
It would be wiser that you spent your time
To gather money for the fire-temple
That will be built at Chala. No king will rise
From that poor broken race of Israel.
No end will come to strife 'twixt Light and Darkness.
If you expect this you are chasing shadows.
Farewell!

RHODASPES: I have no knowledge of these things.
As guardian of the royal treasure, the king
Requires me here. The quest is not for me.
If thou must follow it, why, fare thee well!

ANOTHER: My wife expects a child. I cannot leave.

ANOTHER: And I am ill and quite unfit for hardship.
But I will send one of my men with thee
That he may bring me word how thou dost fare.

ABGARUS: [*Who has lingered after the others*]
My son, it may be that the light of truth
Is in this sign that has appeared to thee.
If this be so, 'twill lead thee to the Prince –
Or it may be a shadow of the light
And lead thee false and far, in empty quest.
But it is better to pursue a shadow
With all thy heart than not to seek at all.
And those who quest must often go alone.
I am too old for travel, but my heart
Shall be companion of thy pilgrimage.
Go in peace!

ARTABAN: Abide in peace, my father.

[*Abgarus leaves. Artaban gathers up the jewels and replaces them in
his girdle. For a time he watches the flame flickering on the altar, then
he crosses the hall and looks out on the heavens.*]
Lo, Jupiter and Saturn blend in glory!
And what glows there below them? Yea, the sign!
The King is coming, and I will go to meet Him.

CURTAIN

ACT II

SCENE 1

[A wilderness scene. Artaban and his servant, Bardya, stand at one side of the stage, supposedly holding their horses.]

ARTABAN: Alas, we have a parasang to go
To reach Borsippa and the caravan –
And both of us with horses nearly spent!
But we must let them drink from this canal
And get their wind.

[They lead their horses two or three paces into the wing.]

BARDYA: What hour is then,
My lord?

[Artaban consults the stars.]

ARTABAN: It is approaching midnight now –
The hour my friends without me should depart.

[A groan is heard.]

But Bardya! Did you hear a sound?

BARDYA: A groan?

[They search here and there. Bardya stops suddenly.]

Here lies a wounded man, my lord. Much hurt,
And bleeding sorely still.

ARTABAN: *[Hurrying over and kneeling]*
He is not dead?
Nay, the heart still flutters in the breast.
He must have been beset by robbers here.
But if we leave him he will surely die.
Do thou then help me! Loosen first his turban.

BARDYA: But, master, if you now delay, your friends –

ARTABAN: Will go without me. Whereas, if here I stay,
With God's help I shall save a human life.

The Prince can live without me. This man, not.
Fetch water, Bardya!
[*He draws his "medicine kit" out of his girdle and holds an herb to the man's nose. The man stirs.*]
Lo, our patient stirs.
How does it happen, you lie wounded here?

HEBREW: I was beset by thieves, then robbed and beaten.
               I surely should have died without your help.
               Who are you then, that showeth such compassion?

ARTABAN: My name is Artaban, from Ecbatana.

BARDYA: He is a Persian Magi, to your fortune.
               Well learned they in all the arts of healing,
               Or else you would ere this be dead.

HEBREW: And I a Hebrew merchant am, from Syria.
               You are indeed a great and noble lord
               To render succor to a helpless man.
               One rarely finds such goodness nowadays –
               Your horses both look tired. Surely I
               Delay you on some mission of importance.

ARTABAN: There is no hurry now. 'Tis sure my friends
               Have gone. I was to meet their caravan
               And journey with them to Jerusalem.
               For to us all, a wondrous star appeared
               As sign that *there* is born the Prince of Peace.
               It is our purpose there to worship Him.

HEBREW: I have no gold to give you, being robbed.
               But if the Prince of Peace is truly born,
               Then I can tell you better where to find him.
               For Hebrew prophets have foretold the birth
               In Bethlehem. 'Tis there that you should go,
               And not Jerusalem. But now, perchance
               Your friends have been delayed as well. Pray go!
               And may the God of Abraham thee guide,
               Because thou hast had pity on the sick!

ARTABAN: You are not well enough to leave, my friend.
               You will need care, indeed for many a moon.
               But, Bardya, we can put him on my horse
               And to Borsippa go together still.

He may be right. Perhaps my friends have waited.

[*They lift the injured man carefully and carry him off stage to where the horses are waiting just out of sight.*]

SCENE 2

ARTABAN: [*Speaking to Bardya who is still off stage*]
Do thou tether the horses, Bardya, there –
And make the Hebrew comfortable as well.
The last rise of the hill I'll climb alone.
[*Hurries a few paces and stops*]
In ghostly gloom the ruined temple lies,
While there the mocking Moon and Jupiter
Indifferent look on. My friends are gone!

[*Bardya enters.*]

BARDYA: No sign of them?

ARTABAN: No sign.

BARDYA: The dawn approaches.
[*Looks westward*]
Perhaps the caravan is still in sight?

ARTABAN: [*Also looking westward*]
Nay, empty marshes stretch to the horizon.
With only here a bittern, there a jackal.

BARDYA: Lo, master, see this cairn of broken bricks!
And under them a piece of parchment rests!

ARTABAN: Give here! [*Reads*] "We have waited past the midnight
And can delay no longer. We must go
To find the King. – Follow if you will."

[*Artaban sits down on the ground and covers his head in despair.*]

BARDYA: A pity! Yet perhaps it is as well.
They all may perish in the desert wastes
And serve at last to feed the vultures there.
In Ectabana thou hast long to live.

ARTABAN: [*Jumps to his feet*]
> The sun has dawned! There is no time to waste!
> In Babylon my sapphire I shall sell
> And buy a train of camels for the journey.
> 'Twill pay for that and for the Hebrew's care,
> And you will bide with him until he's mended.
> I see you have no heart for desert quests,
> But I'll not tarry till I find the King.

CURTAIN

ACT III

[*Bethlehem on the day the slaying of the children has been ordered by Herod. At the left a house. Everything seems empty and quiet.*]

ARTABAN:
> The town appears quite empty and abandoned.
> Silent, except where here and there a dog
> Whimpers and whines, looking for its master.
> And I had thought to find a festival,
> The celebration of a great event,
> Joy and jubilation unrestrained!
> Why, one would think the folk had taken flight!
> The windows and the doors stand open wide,
> As if to mark the emptiness within.
> And yet this house appears inhabited.
> I'll knock and see if anyone be here.

[*He knocks. After a pause, the door is opened a crack. Anna peers out hesitantly.*]

ANNA:
> Whom seek ye, sir? Ye seem to be a stranger.

ARTABAN:
> I seek that Child of worth and wonder rare,
> That King, who should in Bethlehem be born –
> Yet find no one at all to lead me there.

ANNA:
> The Child to Mary and to Joseph born?
> My lord, ye come too late, for they are fled!

[*During the last words, Simon has come out of the house.*]

ARTABAN:
> Are fled? And why? What can have happened then?

SIMON:	Calamitous, the threat that hovers here!
	I will relate the story of the recent days.
	Great wonders hereabout had taken place,
	For truly here the Heaven's Child was born.
	And hither streamed the folk from near and far,
	To worship Him and give Him worthy gifts.
	Yea, even kings with gifts magnificent
	Their homage paid.
ARTABAN:	My friends from far off Persia?
	Were they among the ones to gather round?
ANNA:	Indeed, they found the Child and brought their gifts.
	It was directly after their departure –
	Upon an angel's warning, so they say –
	That Joseph fled with Mary and the Child
	In haste so great, they left their goods behind.
	'Tis said they've gone to far off Egypt's land.
SIMON:	It seemed to all of us an evil sign.
	As if the sun had dimmed to utter darkness.
	And then the rumor spread abroad, the king,
	Because he feared the babe, had made decree
	That soldiers every newborn child should slay.
	'Tis hence the village empty stands. The folk
	Have fled with flocks and herds into the hills,
	In hope that scattering thus far and wide
	Would save their children's lives.
ARTABAN:	And you remain?
ANNA:	Alas, our only child lies very ill!
	He moans and tosses in a fever high.
	Besides, he's three years old – no newborn child.
	We hope they will not harm him, but we know
	He would not live exposed to chills and dew.
	[At first in the distance, then coming closer, shouts and the clanging of weapons are heard.]
SIMON:	They're coming! O, good sir, can you not help us?
	Before a stranger, they might hesitate
	To draw their swords.

ARTABAN:

Go in and I'll endeavor
From your threshold to divert their minds.

[*A group of soldiers, led by a captain, comes on stage making a great commotion. The soldiers scatter into the wings. The captain alone remains. He does not at first notice Artaban in the doorway.*]

CAPTAIN:

What a fine assignment for a soldier!
Invade a dead and quite deserted village
To murder sleeping children – who aren't there!
It seems that Herod must have lost his wits,
To fear a tiny child. And he is old.
The slyest tyrant cannot murder all
Of those who might succeed him to the throne –
The people must have gotten wind of this
Unnatural decree and fled the town.
But that is not my business. My orders are
To kill the kiddies – and orders must be followed.
Although if none I find, none can I kill.
This house here is the last and then we're done.
But who's the foreign fellow standing yonder?
You there! What is your business here! Make way!
I have to enter in that house and search it!

ARTABAN:

I heard your words, O Captain. Believe me,
That one you look for is not in this house.

CAPTAIN: [*Aside*]

Of that I must convince myself.

ARTABAN: [*Removing something from his girdle*]

See here! I hold a ruby, gleaming red –
Worth more than any sword as red with blood.
It could belong to a certain prudent captain –
Who leads his soldiers peacefully away.

[*Soldiers return. Artaban retires into the shadow of the doorway.*]

CAPTAIN:

Have you found some villagers? Or children?

FIRST SOLDIER:

No, sir.

SECOND SOLDIER:

Indeed, we've rummaged all about –

THIRD SOLDIER:

And naught forgotten –

FOURTH SOLDIER:	And naught we've found, sir, either.
FIFTH SOLDIER:	This expedition is considered finished?
CAPTAIN:	It is and you're dismissed. For this house here, I take the full responsibility. The child we seek – he is not here. Break up, And meet again outside the village gate.

[*Soldiers withdraw. Artaban steps forward again.*]

And has my conduct met with your approval?

ARTABAN:	Exactly so. And here is your reward. [*Gives him the ruby*]
CAPTAIN:	Aha! I always fancied gems like this! Now I'll retire, far from Herod's sight, Find some cute wench and live a life of ease – Nor ever be assigned to murder children!
ARTABAN:	Live well!

[*Captain departs.*]

He's not too bad a knave at that –
Alas – the gems I wished to give the King
Are gone for naught – except the silvery pearl.
And yet, the little child whose life was saved
May live to serve the King. It ill behooves
That I should say, God knows not what he doeth
In guiding me to save another's life.
And if I must forever come too late
To find the One I seek – or lacking gifts –
Well, God knows what rewards to mete to all.
The quest I'll not give up, but take the pearl
And go to Egypt, if the road leads there.
I'll find Him there – or seek Him till I die.

CURTAIN

INTERLUDE
[*Select and read paragraphs from Van Dyke on Artaban's next thirty-three years.*]

ACT IV

[A street in Jerusalem on Good Friday. Artaban enters, grown old and bent, leaning on a staff. His clothes are dingy but he still wears a white cap and the winged circle on his breast. Passersby come and go. Then for a moment he is alone.]

ARTABAN: In three and thirty years of wandering,
Full often was I in this city, too,
Searching through its lanes and crowded hovels,
Even in its dark and dingy prisons –
Yet never found the Nazarene I sought.
Still, in my breast today there stirs a feeling,
A joy, as though my quest were nearly ended.
[People are passing, again.]
The others show a strange excitement, too –
But not of joy.
[He stops a group.]
What is the tumult's cause,
And whither do the people hasten so?

PASSERBY: They crucify two robbers and a Jew
At Golgotha, a hill outside the city.

[The group hurries on. Artaban waylays a man walking, alone. It is Simon.]

ARTABAN: Please tell me, who is the Jew they crucify?
And what his crime.
[Looks searchingly at Simon]
Do I not know you, sir?

SIMON: *[Looking carefully at him]*
Indeed you do! I don't forget the man
Who saved my child, and paid a ruby's price!
And now upon another day of woe
We meet again. For it is He you sought
Who faces crucifixion here today
By Pontius Pilate's order.

ARTABAN: Of what accused?

SIMON: Of saying He was King of all the Jews.
Of speaking of Himself as Son of God.
Of healing sick folk on the Sabbath Day.
Of preaching sermons to the multitudes.

And giving poor and heartsick folk some hope.
These are His crimes – and gathering disciples
Whom He taught – my son is one of them
I'm proud to say – and you'll be proud to hear it.
In Bethlehem, the angel saved His life –
But now, no power can intervene. The world
Has turned against Him. His followers are few –
All poor, and helpless to defend His life.

ARTABAN: [*Excitedly*]   The pearl!
Perhaps it's not too late to bring Him that,
And buy His life from mercenary men!

[*As he starts to stride in as much haste as possible on his way, there is a scream from a house and a scuffle in a doorway. A young woman plunges out, followed by a cruel looking innkeeper and some servants.*]

INNKEEPER: Catch the wench! She is my property!

[*The girl, seeing Artaban's white cap and the winged circle on his breast, throws herself at his feet.*]

PERSIAN GIRL: For Ormuzd's sake, protect me from this man!

ARTABAN: [*Stepping between them*]
You call on Ormuzd? I'm a Persian, too,
And will defend you.
[*To the Innkeeper*]
Why do you trouble her?

INNKEEPER: You mind your business! She owes me lots of money,
And I'm not going to let her go for naught.

ARTABAN: How so?

PERSIAN GIRL: Oh lord, my father and I dwelt
In this man's house. My father was a merchant
And never failed to pay his debts on time.
But he fell ill – now many moons ago –
And all the best physicians failed to heal him.
As best I might, I nursed him till he died.
But penniless he died and much in debt,
For rent as well. And now our host intends
To force me into slavery, that I
As servant may work out my father's debts.

ARTABAN: [*To the Innkeeper*] If I should undertake to pay the debt,
                    You'll let the maiden go?

INNKEEPER: From your attire,
                    It looks unlikely you could find so much.

ARTABAN: [*Removes the pearl from his girdle*]
                    See here, the tender luster of this pearl –
                    It shall be hers, to pay her father's debts,
                    And find her way to Persia once again –
                    It was to be the ransom of a King.

INNKEEPER: If you are serious, this suits me well.
                    I'll reckon up the debt and bring the change.

                    [*Exit Innkeeper*]

PERSIAN GIRL: In all my life, I never thought to find
                    Such generosity to a friendless girl
                    And orphaned, from a man unknown to her.
                    May Ormuzd well reward you for your deed!

                    [*Suddenly it grows dark; a rumble is heard in the distance. People run
                    out of their houses in alarm.*]

SIMON: How sinister and dark the daylight grows!
                    An eerie wind is sweeping down the alley.

ARTABAN: A cloud of darkness overwhelms the sun!
                    The Powers of Light themselves must mourn today
                    The dark event at Golgotha fulfilled!
                    Not gloomier it were within a tomb!

                    [*Mighty thunder and quaking*]

FIRST WOMAN: An earthquake!

SECOND WOMAN: Flee! The houses fall!

THIRD WOMAN: Take care!

FOURTH WOMAN: Oh, woe! Your warning came too late, for there
                    The old man lies, struck down by a falling stone.

                    [*Simon and the Persian Girl lean over the fallen Artaban.*]

SIMON: This noble man who failed in life to find
                    The Galilean, by strangest destiny
                    Is bound to Him in death.

PERSIAN GIRL: He is not dead!
                    He breathes – and see! His eyelids flutter, too!

                    [*Artaban raises himself on his elbow and looks past Simon and the
                    girl, as though he beheld a wonder just behind them. They turn and
                    look around, but obviously see nothing.*]

ARTABAN: Nay, King! When have I seen Thee hungry and fed Thee?
                    Or thirsty and gave Thee drink? It is not so!
                    When saw I Thee a stranger and took Thee in?
                    Or naked and clothed Thee? When saw I Thee sick or in prison
                    And came to Thee? For three and thirty years
                    I sought Thee, but never have I seen Thy face
                    Nor ministered to Thee, my King.

                    [*From offstage sounds a voice, clear but not loud – it might well be
                    feminine – while Artaban looks as though he were beholding a vision.*]

VOICE: "Verily I say unto thee, inasmuch as thou hast done it unto one of
                    the least of these My brethren, thou hast done it unto Me."

                    [*Artaban slowly, wonderingly, takes one hand of the Persian Girl and
                    one of Simon.*]

ARTABAN: I've seen the King! I've heard His voice!
                    Already in my life I found Him – and knew it not!
                    [*Artaban slowly sinks back and dies.*]

                                    CURTAIN